Thames Rambler
by Bill Walford
additional photographs by John Palethorpe

Acknowledgements

I would like to thank all those who wittingly or unwittingly helped to inspire or prepare this book - John Palethorpe for the companionship and the photographs, John and David for the comic relief, Adele and Anne for the transport and the nourishment, Frank and Margaret Cuerden for considerable technical assistance and proof reading, Peter Classey for professional advice, and an extra thankyou to Anne who kept nagging me to finish both walk and book.

Completing the walk was the easy bit.....

Printed by Parchment Press, Oxford

Contents

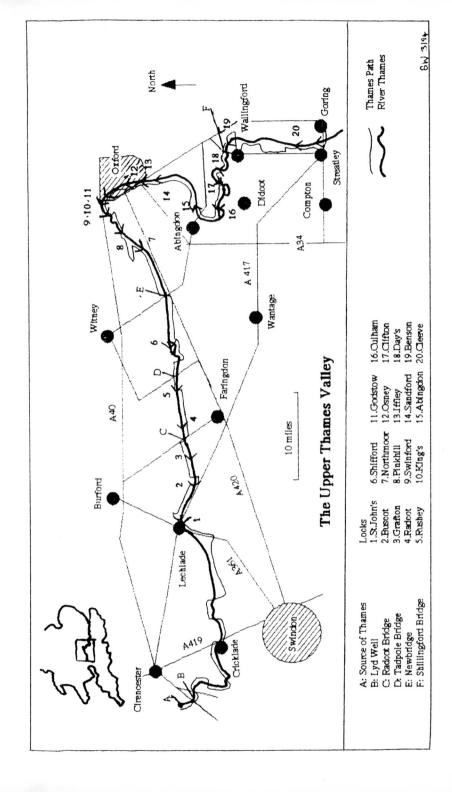

The Upper Thames Valley

North

Cirencester

Burford

Lechlade

Cricklade

Swindon

Witney

Faringdon

Wantage

Didcot

Oxford

Abingdon

Wallingford

Compton

Streatley

Goring

A40
A419
A420
A417
A34
A361

9·10·11
12
13
14
15
16
17
18
19
20

1 2 3 4 5 6 7 8

A: Source of Thames
B: Lyd Well
C: Radcot Bridge
D: Tadpole Bridge
E: Newbridge
F: Shillingford Bridge

Locks
1.St.John's
2.Buscot
3.Grafton
4.Radcot
5.Rushey
6.Shifford
7.Northmoor
8.Pinkhill
9.Swinford
10.King's
11.Godstow
12.Osney
13.Iffley
14.Sandford
15.Abingdon
16.Culham
17.Clifton
18.Day's
19.Benson
20.Cleeve

10 miles

Thames Path
River Thames

BW·3·94

Prelude

Sunday 6th. January
"You need to get fit!", she said.

I never argue with a woman, not even when she catches me off guard. Picture this. I was sitting by the roaring log fire on a chilly January evening, having just finished one of Adele's excellent dinners of the sort where courtesy demands you have three helpings of everything. John had just brought in the Glenfiddich, and was in the act of pouring a tot each when she-who-knows-best came in to the room, saw me slumped near-horizontal in my chair with my eyelids drooping and with my well-filled stomach bulging, and issued her ultimatum.

"Yes, Dear", I said. What else could I say? Spending 40 hours a week cooped up in a car teaching people to drive must be one of the most sedentary yet stressful jobs there is, and so secretly I agreed with she-who-knows-best that I should get more exercise. What she meant of course was getting a dog and taking a daily brisk 5-mile walk, or enthusiastically working out three times a week at the local sports centre. By coincidence (honestly!) earlier that evening John and I had already mulled over the idea of exercise, though on a much grander scale than that proposed by my nearest-and-dearest. Eighteen months had passed since John, my two lads and me had walked the Ridgeway Path (all forty-odd miles of it, by easy stages) in 1989, and we now felt sufficiently rested to consider bigger things. We pondered a bit more over the Glenfiddich. "The Pennine Way?", I said. John contemplated his glass, then smiled and shook his head. "Not that big, mate".

I don't know why I suggested the Thames Path. (There were many moments in the next ten months when my legs hurt or when we got attacked by rampant vegetation that I wished I hadn't.) The more we thought about the project, the more obvious it became that it was perfectly viable. A map confirmed my worst suspicions. The River Thames from its source near Cirencester right down to the Goring gap was all easily accessible, with John living just a few miles from Goring and the whole stretch being within half an hour's drive or so of my Wantage home. Conveniently for us less-than-fit would-be walkers the Upper Thames is crossed by roads every ten miles or so, and ten miles-ish was the sort

1

of distance that we reckoned we could cope with in one day. Better still for us idle chaps, riverside walking would of course be level, easy going.

So that's why, in eight stages over some ten months of 1991, four humans and a dog walked the 85-mile upper section of the Thames Long Distance Path from where the River Thames cuts through the chalk of the Chilterns and Berkshire Downs, upstream to the source in Gloucestershire. Certainly this walk has been done before, certainly it has been written about before, but despite many a hassle and pair of stiff legs on the way, we found it to be something rather special.

By chucking-out time that January night, a daft idea had become a firm project, and we set a provisional date of February 10th. to walk from Goring to Shillingford.

Interlude - 10th-24th. February.

10th. February. 7.30am! I awoke, feeling keen. This was the big day! This was the day planned for my umpteenth effort at getting fit. But no! - a look out of the window indicated that Old Mother Nature saw things differently. I picked up the phone.

"Good Morning, John. How's the weather at your end?".

Not being given to idle and un-necessary chat, John held the phone up to the window so I could see the snowdrifts halfway up his bungalow, whereupon we retired back to our beds. It was to be another two weeks before the snow had cleared properly, and the weather forecasters promised 'a mild day, apart from a chance of a band of showers'.

While the snow clears, let me introduce:
The Players.
Besides being economical in the use of words, John (referred to hereinafter as 'Big' John) is a middle-aged civil servant, a keen vegetable gardener, a brewer of delicious home-made wines, and a countryman at heart. Big John brought as companion Ben-the-Dog, a most aimiable domesticated collie of (almost) unlimited energy.

2

My elder son 'Young' John celebrated his 11th. birthday during the year. Tall, but lightly built, he is naturally inquisitive and very sharp-eyed: he'd like to think he's a trainee David Attenborough. Two-years-younger brother David also has a sharp mind, but directs it differently. He views a long walk in the country as an interruption to his computer games, but I couldn't see any real reason why he shouldn't make the trip, so he found himself dragged along 'for his own good'.

Me? Overweight and under-exercised, I needed to get fit. I am not naturally energetic - even as a teenager I was occasionally referred to as the 'Horizontal Champ'. My knowledge of British natural history was embarrasingly poor to boot ("What's that, Dad?" "A bird, son".), so for the sake of my health, and for the sake of the kids, who couldn't be allowed to grow up as ignorant as I had, we went.

The Logistics.
Thames Path does not lend itself to circular trips, and walking out and retracing steps seems such a waste of effort, that we adopted the 'two cars, two drivers' method that we had used for walking the Ridgeway. This means meeting at a pre-arranged point, driving in convoy to the end point of that day's walk, leaving one car there, and all cramming into the other one to return to the start. At the end of the day's walking, we all cram into the car left conveniently at our destination, then drive back to collect the car that had been left all on its lonesome at the starting point. Simple, isn't it? Of course, there is an easier way. Your chauffeur - or wife - takes you all to the start, and collects you all from the pub at the finish - if you're very lucky!

3

One
"I wish I'd never started"

Goring to Shillingford - Sunday 24th. February

We four chaps and Ben-the-Dog met at the Shillingford Bridge Hotel, leaving one car in the hotel car park which is For Patrons Only. (I had a clear conscience - I had been a patron, in December 1979, and, incidentally, I enjoyed the trout!). Big John drove us to Streatley where he crossed the River Thames to park in a most obscure car park hidden in a twist of Goring. We took a few photographs of each other, and then we took a few deep breaths before we set off. She-who-knows-best was right about me needing to get some exercise - I was beginning to get a bit short of breath after just the three hundred yards back across the Goring-Streatley bridge.

The footpath bypassed a very expensive hotel with jacuzzi and fitness room (how appropriate, I thought!) then wound gently past the church, through a field and over a short length of causeway into the riverside meadows.

The first views of the River Thames on an overcast but mild Sunday morning were very much as I'd imagined they'd be. The fields were of short, damp grass promising the hoped-for level walking. The ground was was quite firm underfoot, and yet, judging by the plague of soft brown spoil-heaps sprouting everywhere, evidently easy digging for a herd of moles.

The fields bordering the Thames are often separated by hedges or substantial fences, with passage provided by walker-friendly gates or stiles. These are generally maintained by the Thames Conservancy, and in this area at least, all of the gates and stiles were in very good repair, freshly painted in grey. Each gate or stile was numbered, with the numbers decreasing as we went upstream, though the numbering seemed to get more random the further we went. A lot of work had also been done on the Goring lock and weir just upstream of the road bridge, leaving it looking very spruce.

In this area, and for most of the river upstream, the footpath sensibly followed the flat route, with the water level generally just a few feet below us. In parts, the bank

4

had crumbled away creating miniature bays, and there were numerous cattle watering places. There was no shortage of birdlife. There were mallards, of course, but there was also a heron, which landed behind a tree and refused to be photographed, and a goose or two, which Young John's spotters' book told us were Canada Geese. We also spotted a very skinny-necked mallard which turned out to be a Great Crested Grebe, the first one I'd ever seen, and yet just the first of several we were to see that day.

We were barely under way when we were accosted by two teenage girls who, having already mountained-biked their way past, returned to ask most politely, "Please, can we keep going and cross the river further up?" Their accents betrayed them as foreigners, but they displayed the usual foreigner's faultless English. In faultless yokel-speak we explained that we didn't know where the nearest crossing was, but they could certainly cross some seven miles about ("seven divide by five times eight equals... oh...") eleven kilometres onwards at Wallingford. "Eleven kilometres?!!?" "Yes". A pause - they looked at each other - "OK, thankyou". This was another thing that betrayed them as foreigners - a conversation! Had they been British, two teenage girls would have totally ignored us. These two departed enthusiastically on their bikes. We assumed they found what they wanted as we never saw them again.

The first serious puddle of the day showed how easy it is to waste a tenner. Wellies are not quite the approved footwear for serious walking, so I had lately bought David a pair of substantial trainers-cum-boots, certainly very comfortable, though unfortunately in gleaming white. David gaily inserted his new trendy white boots into the water. Were David's new trendy white boots water resistant? NO! This was not David's day. There couldn't have been more leaks if it had been St. David's Day. Luckily for him we joined a tarmac road leading to Cleeve Lock, which gave his boots and feet a bit of a chance to dry.

The entrance gate to Cleeve lock itself seemed stuck, and, having struggled with it a while, we heard a voice. "Oi!", it said. We looked round to see who was being shouted at. "You two, you two chaps with the kids and dog!". Us? We looked up to see the lock-keeper looking despairingly at the sight of four apparently incompetent walkers trying to open the access gate to his lock. "It opens the other way!" Eyes averted, we slunk rapidly through his domain.

Upstream of the lock there were several large flocks of Canada geese. They are very skillful fliers for such big birds. Unlike your average sparrow, large birds

5

cannot reach flying speed instantly, and I found it fascinating to watch them accelerate as they took off, and accelerate more as they built up to cruising speed. Canada geese have a well-deserved reputation for being noisy birds - or perhaps its just that flying off the Thames needs a lot of instructions from the bird traffic controllers. Other birds were trying to get in on the act too, though the sound of a skylark singing falls much more kindly on the ear than the honking of geese. The lark's song, together with a large quantity of rooks cawing in the trees on the opposite bank, was another link with our previous expedition. To me, the combination of skylark song and rook calls is the typical sound of the Ridgeway.

After two miles or so of fields and geese the footpath came to an end, there being no right of way through a series of private riverside properties at Moulsford and beyond. The path terminated in the courtyard of the 'Beetle and Wedge' which is like a lot of riverside pubs, with its moorings and terrace, and consisting of a number of scattered buildings. We bumped into a young chef carrying a plate of fresh-fried bubble-and-squeak. The smell wafting from this plate was just the thing to get the taste buds started and the brain fantasising, especially after a couple of miles walking on a grey morning like this. But this was no time for a rest - the pub wasn't even open yet, dammit! - and so we regretfully kept going up a lane to join the main A329 through Moulsford.

This is where doubt and disillusion started to creep in. As far as I was concerned, I'd already had enough exercise for one day - a couple of miles of tolerable country walking and a little wildlife-spotting was more than enough excitement for one day. Unfit as I was, my muscles were already beginning to complain, and I wasn't keen on the idea of many miles still to go. The guidebook we had chosen, which I wouldn't recommend to anybody, would have us believe that the track back down to the river would be within a mile of the 'Beetle and Wedge'. So, we were faced with at least a mile of walking alongside a narrow and fast main road. 'Within a mile', it said. Don't believe it. We couldn't find it. We walked a good two miles and more along the roadside footpath before we finally came to a way back down to the Thames. The track that most nearly matched the guidebook's description showed evidence that an irate landowner had already suffered from too many previous walkers along the side of his field. A whole string of notices confronted us: 'Private', 'No Entry', 'No Access to River', 'Our Fido Will Bite You and Tear You into a Thousand Pieces'. We took the hint.

This really was a gloomy two miles. Somewhere along the Moulsford main street we must have passed the house that had been the scene of a recent I.R.A. bomb

6

attempt. Beyond the village we plodded past the defunct garage and pub 'available for development', past some depressingly untended, overgrown allotments - on and on we went. We passed the Fairmile Hospital. 'There is no Accident or Casualty service at this Hospital'. Well, there wouldn't be at a mental hospital, would there? Is it just tact that prevents the Authority from labelling it for what it is? There had been plenty of evidence along the roadside of those who perhaps should be committed to the Fairmile - it would almost be possible to start a spares dealership with the bits and pieces of broken car scattered along the verges.

Despite the gloom and despondency, two miles from Goring became three miles and eventually four miles - a lot of distance for a normally-sessile object like me. David, never an enthusiastic walker at the best of times, started to struggle a bit - and made a point of letting us know. 'My legs hurt.' 'Can we have a rest?' 'Is it time for dinner?' Like David's, my legs were really starting to complain, too, though I didn't dare say so. I envied Big John's steady, slow, long stride - he never seemed to tire. Young John, luckily for him, has a great deal of stamina. Maybe his legs hurt just as much as mine, but he was enjoying the walk, and was forever finding something of interest to see.

We detoured slightly into a lay-by, just as a car pulled up. Could we direct him to the Shillingford Bridge Hotel? "Shush!", I said, pointing to David. "If he hears you I shall have a mutiny on my hands". Very quietly, I sketched the driver a silent map, keeping an eye on David to make sure he didn't find out what was going on. I was unusually kind to the driver, hoping he would still be at the hotel to buy us a drink when (or if) we arrived.

The detour into the layby was fortunate, for leading off it was a track that we could use to get back to the Thames. But first I had to give in to the mutterings from the most junior child and let him take a breather. Let's be honest - it suited me to take a break, too. Perching on an old gate in the shelter of a hedge, looking at the field in front of me and trying to ignore the grey and depressing layby and traffic behind me, I was of the opinion that, so far, this walk had been a disappointment.

Having breathered, we set off down the track which ran along the edge of a field. At the bottom we wriggled through the spiky bushes, carefully edged round a deep pond without slipping in, and, at last, found our way over a bank and another field back to the Thames. Surely it was time for lunch?

We found ourselves a sheltered spot near the river and perched as best we could.

One of the pleasures of walking is to be away from all the daily hassle - in my case to be away from cars and telephones. A light lunch in my pocket makes me feel completely independent of the routine haste of the world, and a simple ham roll, bag of crisps and a swig of water made an excellent snack. Now, had Big John brought his water-and-whiskey refresher? Yes he had! Good lad! This hip flask had appeared without fail at critical moments on our Ridgeway trip. A small swig is remarkably refreshing, though Young John doesn't like the taste of whiskey. David doesn't like it either, but he keeps working on it.

The combination of the whiskey and being back alongside the Thames made the day feel less gloomy, and I started to take an interest in our surroundings. We discussed why there should still be concrete pill boxes along the bank. Dating back to the summer of 1940, they were built as a second line of defence against a possible invasion by Hitler's chaps, forming what was known as the GHQ. Line. Today they don't seem to be used by anyone for anything - is it just too much trouble to remove them, or are they seen as a monument to the Home Front? In this area there are pillboxes on both sides of the river - perhaps the Home Guard didn't know if it was coming or going.

Across the river was another pair of Great Crested Grebes, diving under for fish, presumably, and then surfacing again some distance away. They were lovely to watch, but I don't see how such a skinny fowl can justify being called a 'Great' anything. If there is a Lesser Crested Grebe it must be a very insignificant beast. And scattered around us we had the Fishermen, clearly identified by labels on their clothing and gear as Timothy Trout, or 'Chubby' Smith, after the style of Hell's Angels. These chaps were the remnants of a fishing contest - and don't they take it seriously! The effort that goes in to these contests is beyond me. Most of the fisher persons we passed were kitted out with many a rod, plus nets, baskets and boxes full of gear, necessitating a large off-road trolley to transport it all. It strikes me as out of all proportion to the fish they might catch - most of which go back into the water anyway.

I inspected David's soggy, useless, off-white boots and saturated socks, and his feet. Despite the soaking, and the eczema he suffered from then, there was no sign of cracking, nor of sores. So, considerate Daddy that I am, I dried his feet, put a good dollop of Vaseline on them, wrung out and replaced his socks, and got the indescribable pleasure of re-lacing his soggy, muddy boots for him. I took one more well-deserved swig of water-and-whiskey; then refreshed and feeling more optimistic, we were off.

8

The path, narrow at this point, led through the riverside woods which bordered a good mile of broad, straight river. Young John, gangly child that he can be at times, stumbled on an uneven footbridge crossing a tiny tributary, and so we other three drew lots to see who should ask him if he 'enjoyed the trip'. I won!

We left the woods behind and entered a series of more open meadows, one of which appeared to contain an aeroplane parked at its far side. On closer inspection we discovered that the field doubled as a grass airstrip, marked at one end with a windsock. The aeroplane was a single-engined high-wing Cessna something, but what model it might have been I can't say. Despite having flown several variants, I really can't tell a 150 from a 152 from a 172. I also had my doubts about getting any light aircraft airborne from this short length of airstrip - I'm certain the Grob motorglider that I normally fly would struggle to take off safely from it. I also wondered about a private owner operating so close to RAF Benson, home of the Queens Flight - I wondered if the Queen knew about this strip?

On the approach to Wallingford the path cut across a number of back gardens. Some owners had fenced off our path; some, having more faith in human nature, had merely marked the footpath and had put us on trust not to stray into their private parts. Then, with the road bridge at Wallingford in sight, the riverside path came to an end in a large boatyard, looking rather forlorn and unloved on a grey winter's afternoon, with little bits and pieces of boatmongery scattered around. A number of boats were for sale, but they were frighteningly expensive. £5000 barely buys you a small, tatty 2-berth cruiser - and the outboard engine will be extra.

We followed the footpath leading us away from the Thames and out in to the back alleys of Wallingford. Big John said that he finds Wallingford an unspoilt town that has not been 'messed about too much in the middle'. That's probably because, until the very recent opening of the relief road, the traffic was so often solidly jammed up that no developer would have had elbow room to swing a sledge hammer.

We didn't seem to have the inclination to stroll around this unspoilt town, but merely trudged onward along the streets to the long, single track bridge over the Thames. Halfway across Young John and David found some seats set into the stonework, and demanded another break to give them a chance to work at the remains of their rations. Big John and I had a Kit-Kat and a committee meeting. The guidebook said the route now followed the left bank 'if Benson lock is open'.

9

But, if it wasn't, then it would have meant a two-mile walk there to find out, and a two-mile walk back to Wallingford again to cross the Thames over this very same road bridge if it wasn't. We were in no mood for taking chances. The light was already fading, the weather was turning chilly, and neither of us fancied risking an extra hour's struggle. We settled for the boring road route running parallel to the right bank.

Having followed the line of the old Oxford road past the large Institute of Hydrology with its long beech hedge all brown and autumny, even in February, the suggested route was through Preston Gifford, where we assumed we would rejoin the river bank. Annoyingly, having passed a number of cottages with optimistic names like 'Ferry Cottage' and 'Waterside' and 'Private Access' we found ourselves almost back on the Oxford road again three quarters of a mile later! Still, Benson lock was at hand, and we were very pleased to find we had made the correct choice back at Wallingford - there had been no river crossing available at the lock.

We were, at last, able to get back to the river bank, and after 'one last rest' on a tempting bench under a tree, I dragged both flagging lads to their feet, and jollied them along for the final stretch, promising soft, jolly green meadows and no more hard roads. But nothing in life is ever simple, is it? Not far into the meadows David's sweet little voice called to me. "Dad, I think my flask has fallen out".

I didn't swear, I didn't yell. Despite my tired and aching legs, I simply bowed to the inevitable and retraced the path back towards Benson lock. A quarter mile back in a previous field, lying just a yard to the rear of an uncaring fisherman and fortunately just clear of a cowpat, was a bright blue object, oblivious to all the pain and agony it had caused me. I picked it up without disturbing either fisherman or cowpat, and struggled to join the others who had wandered quietly onwards. Catching them up was not easy - although they had gone but slowly, my legs were stuck in low gear and simply refused to go faster than a plod. Finally overhauling them, I handed David his flask saying Nothing, very, very loudly.

At last, there came the point where we we could make out Shillingford Bridge, giving us perhaps half a mile to go, and so putting a little heart back in to us. The far bank was quite steep and heavily wooded, and another heron took its chance to play hide and seek with us in and out of the woods, before disguising itself as a tree where Big John still couldn't get a photo of it.

We were, at last, able to get back to the river bank, and after 'one last rest' on a
We tripped and slipped gaily along the tree-lined muddy final few hundred yards
to the bridge, thinking all our troubles were over. But the bridge didn't have a footpath, so crossing it turned out to be the most dangerous stretch of the entire day's
walk, with a lot of traffic very close to our elbows. Muddily, wearily, stiffly we
plodded into the hotel car park. There was no sign of the chap who I'd so carefully
directed to this hotel some hours before. In any case, much as we could have used
a drink, I doubted if this 'For Patrons Only' hotel would want our patronage
dressed as we were in our muddy walking gear.

Big John laughingly pointed out the start of the next section of the Thames Path
just across the river. That could wait. This first stretch had been a good ten miles
long, taken well over five hours, and we had walked as many miles of roads as we
had riverside meadows. As an introduction to what we hoped was going to be a
wonderful series of walks, the combination of indifferent weather and some
tedious diversions had made the Goring - Shillingford stretch of the Thames a most
disappointing event. And as for getting fit, I don't think it did much for me at all.
I was simply knackered. It was nice to find out that Big John was knackered too.

Two
This is Spring?

Shillingford to Abingdon - Sunday 7th. April

David was obviously unimpressed by the idea of long-distance walking and appeared determined to avoid any more. We'd already had to postpone one attempt at this section when he had quite a nasty attack of asthma. Cunningly, he'd managed to have another one just 24 hours before the re-scheduled day - a relatively mild attack, certainly, but enough to make his participation dubious. And no, on the Sunday he wasn't fit enough to go. He seemed to contain his disappointment quite well. Young John also had a minor upset the day before - David had inadvertently eaten the smokey bacon crisps that Young John had chosen for his lunch!

The forecast for the day's walk was typically spring-like - blustery showers and strong winds. So, I packed cagoules and overtrousers, as well as a little food and a few mints, and a separate bag of spare shoes, socks and trousers for Young John. Anne graciously cancelled her plans for the day to baby-sit David, and also agreed to drive us to the start point. We picked up Big John and Ben-the-Dog from Abingdon just after 10.00am, and a mere fifteen minutes drive got us to the Shillingford Bridge Hotel. Things hadn't changed - this car park was still For Patrons Only.

"Is that everything then, dearest?" she said. Ben-the-Dog had made an early start on the bird watching but very swiftly retreated when the swan he was watching took violent and noisy objection to him. "Oh, yes...thankyou", said I, distracted by the kerfuffle. Off she drove, my carefully-packed bag of spare clothing disappearing back to Wantage along with a wife and cheerfully-waving younger son. If we did get wet, we were going to stay that way. Still, undaunted, we tromped gaily over Shillingford Bridge with no footpath yet.

We'd dispensed with our original less-than-helpful guidebook to the Thames Path, and had put our faith in the Ramblers Association guidebook. Experience was to show that this book was an accurate and generally easily-followed guide. It was invaluable on later stages, and rarely let us down. Big John had turned it into travellers' map form, so with Young John 'navigating', we went down a Private Road, and yes, there was a gate and footpath just where it should be. The weather forecast was turning out to be accurate, too - the first gusty shower of rain found us with only another 9.75 miles to go. Thankfully it was brief, but fun while it lasted. A short stroll through the back alleys and past the old farms of Shillingford village brought us out on to the main A423, notorious for its road traffic collisions. Luckily, after only 300 yards or so of very wary pavement walking, the guidebook directed us in to a field and down to the river proper, promising that on this section of the walk we would stay with the river the whole distance.

And, suddenly, the sun shone! This sudden burst of spring sunshine totally changed the day and lifted our spirits. Memories of the disappointing previous walk were still with us, but the combination of sun and a promise of 'no more roads' made us feel much more optimistic. And, for once, our optimism was justified - in retrospect this field marked the point where the pleasurable walking really started. Not that it was all easy...

The intermittent bright spells meant that, despite the river bank being essentially flat and easy walking country, there really was an ever-changing view. Time and again on this walk a change of light, or a change of perspective as we rounded a slight curve, made the whole river look different. With much of the Thames Valley being level and low lying, we could often see miles of wide open countryside.

On the river itself, there were one or two great crested grebes and a pair of mallards to be seen, while the sky above was bright blue in parts, though with many a thick dark cloud bubbling up. I explained to Young John how a storm produces its own local weather, and how the wind direction varies around a storm. Big John expressed a polite interest in what I was saying, so I gave him the whole explanation of the way the weather works in springtime. "I didn't know that", he said.

The river skirted around Dorchester, with the impressive Dorchester Abbey (and some less impressive council houses) lit by the bright sunlight, clearly visible to our right. Dorchester is an ancient town, dating back to Roman times and earlier, and was one of England's most important towns in its day. Big John said the Abbey is nice, though plain, and that the town is unspoilt by tourists.

13

We reached the point where the River Thame joins the River Thames. The River Thames is called (by those in the know) the Isis as it passes through Oxford. The best explanation I've heard for this is that ancient maps marked the river at London as the River Thamesis. OK so far? Now, the River Thame rises in Buckinghamshire and flows roughly south west to join the Thamesis at Dorchester. So, if the two rivers added together form the Thamesis, take away Thame and what have you got? The River Sis. Close enough, isn't it? Arguably, then, upstream from this point on, we were walking along the Isis footpath. Just a matter of labels? Wait and see.

We crossed the footbridge that spans the mouth of the River Thame, pausing in the middle to lean on the rail and contemplate the infinite. The River Thame brought to my mind memories of happy days working at the Gateway superstore (now taken over by Asda), sited in an out-of-the-way spot some miles outside Oxford at Wheatley. The site stands on the west bank of the Thame, and one of the strange benefits of the Gateway company buying such an obscure site was that, to the delight of many of the young lads we employed, we acquired the fishing rights to a quarter mile of River Thame bank.

South of us, forming the far bank, were Little Wittenham Clumps, the highest points of the Sinodun Hills. The clumps are a pair of tree-tufted local beauty spots and viewpoints which none of us had climbed, in spite of the alleged breathtaking view from the top. I was more interested in another footbridge that was just visible in the distance. Though A.A. Milne set his 'Winnie the Pooh' stories in Sussex's Ashdown Forest, the footbridges at Day's lock have become the venue of the Annual World Poohsticks Championships.

My thoughts were interrupted by a sudden Whoosh! as a stony-faced walking enthusiast came striding up behind us in full regulation dress. We barely had time to say 'Good Morning' before he zapped past us. Still, he did us a favour, because he reached Day's lock well before us, thus risking the embarrassment of having to re-trace steps if the path over the lock and weir wasn't open to the public - we waited to see. The lock-keeper let him pass (though at that enthusiastic pace the speed merchant would have taken some stopping!) and so we ambled over, said 'Good Morning', and yes, the weir can be used by the public any time the lock is manned.

This was my first meeting with Lynn David. He is as Welsh as his name suggests, and gifted with that country's vocal skills. As befits the organiser of the

Poohsticks Championships, he's very outgoing, full of tales, and had a comment or two about people who try to take boats on the river in strong cross winds. This arose from a pleasure craft hirer who had that morning been blown on to a mudflat just upstream of the lock. Lynn was not nasty, more pitying of novices who wouldn't take advice. By this time, Captain Halibut had freed his craft from the mud, and brought it in to the lock, giving us a perfect demonstration of how to all but fall in using the 'horizontal bridge position' - two hands on the boat, two feet on the bank.

Lynn David bears some of the responsibility for this book - though he doesn't know it! It was like this. I took both lads to the Poohsticks Championships in January 1993, and spoke briefly to Lynn David then to arrange for a group of children from David's primary school to interview him for their school newspaper - as well as organising the Poohsticks Championship, Lynn had been awarded the B.E.M. in the 1993 New Year's Honours. February's interview turned out to be an all-afternoon fascinating one-man talk about the Thames, the Tourists and the Poohsticks. Somewhere along the way Lynn was talking about the glories of the Upper Thames - he has worked all the locks from St. John's at Lechlade down to this one. "It's a shame no one's written a book about the Upper Thames ", said he "it's the best bit of all".

We took a bit of a rest on the weir, allowing ourselves to be mesmerised by the violent rush of water below, then wriggled through gates and willows to join the meadows on the west bank of the Thames, heading northwards. Little Wittenham Clumps were now behind us, Dorchester Abbey was still visible on the far bank, and everyone's favourite landmark started to peep over the horizon to the west - Didcot Power Station!

The river meadows were very low lying, with mudflats some distance away in the Didcot direction that were still waterlogged from recent flooding. A pair of birds, too small and too rapid to be identified, flashed by and landed among the pools of water. We could hear a skylark or two, but as usual, I couldn't spot them. I watched the peewits/lapwings/plovers that were also gathered on the mudflats. I read somewhere that they are indifferent flyers. Don't believe it. They are amazing beasts in the air, with big broad wings, and an ability to reverse a turn very quickly. A favourite trick is to close the wings, roll inverted, and then fall inverted before recovering near the ground - courtship, or the love of flying? Also airborne was a light plane passing very slowly overhead. His slow progress westward, despite large earfuls of engine, indicated a very strong headwind of

15

30 to 40 knots, and a warning of very changeable weather still to come.

As we rounded the long leftward curve in the river, we lost sight of Dorchester, and saw instead the expensive, expansive gardens of Burcot sweeping down to the water. They looked very nice, but neither Big John nor me fancied the idea of owning and mowing a football pitch-sized lawn, nor could we afford to pay anyone else to do it. From a distance at least, these huge gardens appeared well-tended - either the owners have plenty of time on their hands, or plenty of money.

Talking of plenty of money, we watched one or two pleasure cruisers going upstream, not making much headway against wind and current. I enjoy cruising along a river, but actually owning a river cruiser has always struck me as a very poor investment - these expensive, over-equipped cruisers seem to spend most of their time tied up and ignored. Neither was Big John over-impressed. "I can't see the point", he said. "You cruise up the river, say to Lechlade, then you turn round and cruise back again...".

Big John was impressed by the bird life. At one moment he stood transfixed, camera ready, drooling over the sight of three swans landing in formation on the water. Impressive birds they were, though their passing created a strange creaking noise as they flapped over our heads. They must be very marginal flying devices, with a very poor power-to-weight ratio and a very heavy airframe. And not easy to land either - we watched a youngster fail to lower his undercart in time and come to a very bumpy stop. Noticing that we were distracted, a heron teased us with a stately flypast, then just as Big John spotted him and swung his camera towards the beast, it switched on its afterburner, went into terrain-hugging mode and landed in the next field well out of camera range. Are all herons camera-shy?

We started to meet a handful of strolling persons dressed in Sunday best coming the other way. Now this comes as quite a shock when you're in boots and waterproofs - it's a bit of a jolt to find the real world still exists. It happened to me once on Exmoor, when I was 'leading' a party of cadets on a walk. Frankly, we were lost, believed ourselves to be miles from anywhere, and were simply heading south on the basis that this would eventually bring us to a main road. Coming around the rocks on the desolate, isolated stretch of moorland were two ladies in headscarves, tight skirts and high heels...

16

We were nearing Clifton Hampden, home of the famous Barley Mow pub, as mentioned in Jerome K. Jerome's 'Three Men in a Boat'. One of the great advantages of being a walker is the freedom to have a drink in a remote country pub without worrying about drink-drive laws. There was no chance of either big John or me driving for hours yet, so the pub promised to be the ideal place for lunch. Walking a little further round the bend of the Thames brought Clifton Hampden bridge into sight; a nicely proportioned pointy-arched brick bridge. Sensing the pub, I spotted the steps at the far side of the field leading up to the road, and turned away from the river bank to take a direct line across the field. Young and Big John followed. Unfortunately, also taking a direct line across the field, craftily hidden from view, was a deep and fast-flowing stream between us and the steps. We backtracked to the river bank to follow the proper path, crossing the stream by a thoughtfully-provide footbridge - sorry about the detour, chaps!

At last we reached the pub via the steps and a brisk dash along the road. Big John handed me some cash while he stayed outside with Young John and Ben-the-Dog. Young John would not be persuaded to mind the Ben for an hour while Big John and I went inside and warmed ourselves, so we were all four stuck with sitting outside. Sometimes these eleven-year-old chaps have no feelings.

Bearing in mind the advice of Jerome K. Jerome that, due to low beams and odd levels, this pub is not a place for tall heroines or drunken men, I made my way very carefully to the bar. It really is an old building, and there's no sign of the fire that destroyed the roof not so many years ago. But old pub or not, the prices are bang up-to-date - Young John's double orange juice didn't leave us much change out of a fiver.

If anyone remembers taking lunch at the Barley Mow on Sunday, 7th. April 1991, they may also remember the cabaret provided by three men and a dog. While the diners sat warm and snug at their tables in the pub, treating themselves to the roast beef and gravy that we could only smell, they were also treated to the sight of us sitting in the garden, dressed in our full Arctic gear of boots, cagoules and gloves, cheerfully ignoring a bitingly cold wind suddenly coming down from a threatening black cloud mass. Well insulated against the conditions, we supped orange juice, best bitter and Guinness, munched cheerfully on pies and sandwiches, and commented on the delightful pink blossom on the trees. A flock of twenty or more sparrows kept us amused (and bemused) in our turn by repeatedly leaping out of the hedge, pecking at nothing obvious on the ground, and then all dashing back to the hedge again.

Eating and drinking completed, Young John and Big John made their way to the toilets across the road. I took the tray of glasses back in to the bar, for a last warm, and for a last sniff at the roast beef. In doing so I banged my head on one of the low beams.

Then came the hard bit. Due to my advancing years and my bio-rhythms I find it difficult to get going again after a lunch-break - stiff legs, a full tum and an affinity for the siesta are not conducive to walking. So this time I'd tried consuming a relatively light lunch - just a pork pie and half a pint of Guinness - hoping that with an un-full tum I would go along a little easier. We crossed Clifton's narrow bridge, the two Johns leading, me trying my best to loosen up stiffened muscles, and all three of us hiding in the pedestrian slots from the traffic that whipped past. As he got down to the riverbank Young John, sharp-eyed as ever, spotted a kingfisher. He called out to me, forcing me to rush down a flight of steps to the riverbank just in time for me to see a little streak of blue departing upstream. That was the first kingfisher either of us had ever seen.

We passed Clifton lock, and then went along the straight Clifton cut that clips off the winding, un-navigable loop of the Thames at Long Wittenham, often used as moorings by large numbers of cruisers. A few hundred yards ahead of us an ominous dark mass seemed to be covering the footpath. From our position it looked as though a large herd of cows were blocking our way, though I tried to keep going without letting my fear of these beasts show. My bravery was rewarded, for as we got closer we saw an insubstantial fence just keeping a footpath clear along the bank. Good! - I didn't fancy mixing it with a load of dung-covered bovines. Ben-the-Dog was put on the lead as his sheepdoggy instinct is to herd any animals. The converse of this is that a herd of cows tends to gang up on him, and to move towards the danger. Big John tried to assure me that this ever-growing gang of cows was harmless, but I reckoned there was about 40 tons of harmlessness closing up against that fence, and if they didn't actually trample me, the pollution could well be terminal.

Sneaking past the cows, we came to the end of the cut where the natural line of the river bends sharply, the river level being controlled by a weir. Another heron stood in the water, framed by two of the weir supports. Was this one allergic to cameras? - you bet! one rustle of Big John's camera pocket, and the heron sneaked away, keeping low to avoid radar.

A small sandy beach had formed on the outside of the bend, with an awful lot of human debris washed up on it. All manner of human mess had found its way into the poor old Thames: bread trays, milk crates, and a good dozen traffic cones! Surprisingly, there was no supermarket shopping trolley - though perhaps I missed it. Young John cracked the Green child's joke of the day: 'What stick isn't bio-degradeable? Plastic!'. Plastic may be one of the most versatile of modern materials, but no-one seems to know how to get rid of it. Tree after tree all along the river had its piece of tattered plastic caught up in its lower branches - are there kids out there that believe plastic does grow on trees?

In a field further along our way there appeared to be a lot more white plastic scattered around - bird-scarers maybe? No, closer inspection showed the whiteness to be thirty-odd swans, roosting in the field. Bearing in mind Ben-the-Dog's earlier encounter with a swan, he went back on the lead and we drifted past very quietly. Luckily these swans were not aggressive. Wild life is all very well, but I prefer a good stout fence separating them from me.

Did I mention the wind? This stretch had us going directly into the wind, which was becoming distinctly strong and gusty at times. What with the headwind and a tum full of pie and Guinness, I'd reached the stage where a pleasant walk was becoming a bit of a grind. We had another rest, finding what shelter we could behind some skinny waterside bushes.

Young John said he had been getting chilled. It is unusual to hear any complaint from Young John. He enjoys walking, he enjoys being out for a day, and is not given to whinging, so I took this complaint about being chilled seriously, and gave him a pair of nylon overtrousers from my bag. These did a good job of keeping the wind off him all the way up to his armpits. He was surprised how much difference the extra layer made, though the extra wind resistance of these baggy trousers slowed him down even more.

The Thames Path goes under Appleford railway bridge, built, I believe, as a replacement for I.K.Brunel's original wooden bridge. The present bridge is certainly not one of Brunel's artistic creations - it's probably the sort of iron girder bridge no-one would admit to designing. It's functional enough, a twin-track bow-arched construction, maybe just eight feet above the bank level, and made mainly of rivets held together by strips of iron. Big John said how one of his school pals had gone to work as a 'cherry chucker'. "What's a cherry chucker?", said Young John, so Big John had to explain about riveting, and the way that the red-hot rivets are thrown up from the furnace to the riveters. This particular collection of chucked cherries looked a little the worse for wear on close inspection, with some noticeable rust and flaking paint. Society in the past had cash enough to build railways and the necessary bridges; today we don't even seem to have the cash to keep this bridge in reasonable order.

Another quarter mile or so got us as near as we were going to get to the highlight of the day's walk - we passed by the cooling water intake for Didcot Power Station, with the chimney and the six cooling towers barely a mile away! No doubt about it, this concrete mass dominates the whole of the Upper Thames valley, and although in some ways its stark industrial shapes are totally out of character with the farmlands of the valley, I often think how flat and uninteresting the valley would be without this piece of sculpture sat in the middle.

Didcot Power Station can be seen for miles. Come west down the M40 from London through the deep chalk cutting above Stokenchurch and there it is. Approach along the A40 east from Gloucester and, before you get to Burford, gosh, there it is again. Come up many of the routes leading north over the Berkshire Downs and it's like a lighthouse welcoming you home. The power station's size is deceptive: I know the chimney is over 600 feet high, the cooling towers are in excess of 300 feet tall, but on such a flat vale there's nothing to compare them with. I went in to one of the cooling towers on the last Open Day there. It was just a thin concrete shell, over three hundred feet of it, floor area enough for a football pitch or two, and a totally disorienting view up through the hole at the top.

The wind had continued to gust, and we suffered a heavy shower or two, which made walking both hard and miserable. It was made more miserable by Big John, drawing on hidden reserves of strength, having the cheek to get ahead of us and then turn to take a photo of Young John and me battling mightily with the wind and rain. The walking was made harder still by an unexpected slope upwards on the approach to Culham, where the path rises to quite a height above the river, one of the few places on the whole 85 miles where this was the case.

A field on our bank had signs warning us to 'Keep Out - Rifle Range', which was much more effective than 'No Trespassers'! There was also a cottage, long disused, or maybe it was the arch of a bridge, even longer disused, and bricked up to form a dwelling - we really couldn't tell. At last the Culham cut appeared, then the two Culham bridges, and we crossed the road to flop into weary repose on a sheltered seat just upstream of Culham lock.

Ribena for Young John, water-and-whiskey for Big John and me, and all three of us were relieved to be sheltered from the wind for a spell. Having recovered a little we had strength enough to take in the charm of the very neatly-kept lock. On the opposite bank was a mark for the flood levels of 1947, and an even higher mark for the flood of 1800-and-something. I was unimpressed - I reckoned it was a mere four feet above the current water level at the top of the lock. I told the tale of the River Avon at my old home town of Evesham being eleven feet above normal in the summer of 1968, so high that we couldn't cross the river to get to school. That's what I call a flood.

I tried to encourage Young John by telling him it was only another two miles to the finish. Culham cut, the second significant cut in this area, is tree-lined on the southern bank, which gave a little shelter from the wind, and we opted for the direct and sheltered route along the cut rather than sticking purist-fashion to the longer riverside route via Sutton Courtenay. Even so, the cut took us on a long wide sweep round Culham village, and not until we rejoined the river proper and turned northwards did we finally get the wind on our backs. Young John, usually so full of go, was starting to flag badly, looking unusually pale and un-chirpy for him. It had been a wise decision to leave David at home - he really would have been pushed to cope with the wind.

The riverside path to the west of Culham goes between some youngish willows, and was rather marshy near the water's edge. Some parts of this long distance path are going to erode very quickly once it becomes popular, and I can imagine traffic jams of people in some of these narrow bits. The path threatened to join the boring and fast A415 into Abingdon, but luckily turned across a large wooden footbridge over Swift Ditch. This was the original course of the Thames in days of yore until the monks of Abingdon decided to divert the river nearer to their dwelling. The river's main flow now passes the town: Swift Ditch merely takes any overflow.

The footbridge allowed us an excellent view of a disused stone bridge also crossing Swift Ditch, the purpose of which totally escaped me as it both starts and ends in a field. Unusually for us, we didn't linger long in the middle of this

21

footbridge - the wind was causing it to sway too much for comfort.

The footbridge also gave us access to the series of level meadows that leads in to Abingdon. The new marina, then un-occupied, was of a decent size, but Big John was critical of the architecture of the adjoining new houses on the opposite bank. Maybe someone had tried to create a feeling that the houses had been there a long time, and that their individual design and deliberate uneven roofline had occurred naturally. We thought it just looked tatty. Further upstream, I pointed out the iron bridge with the name of the Wilts. and Berks. Canal Co. on it, and also the recess in the far bank that shows where the canal once joined the Thames. Big John spotted the adjacent old alms houses near St. Helen's church and found that this ancient row of homes was much more pleasing to his eye.

We finally staggered into Abingdon's riverside park. As a treat for completing such a demanding walk, we allowed ourselves the delight of deviating a few yards from the river bank and going direct to the car park. I was glad Big John was driving us home - I don't think I could have driven at that moment. Young John was shattered, and fell asleep in the back of the car.

I took one last look back at the Thames Valley as Big John drove up towards the Downs on the A34. The whole day's walk, and more, could be seen in one glance, from downstream of Wallingford, around Wittenham Clumps, past the power station and on and beyond the spire of St. Helen's church at Abingdon. What one glance couldn't show was the detail and the variety of the Thames riverbank. Despite being knackered (again!), despite the wind and the rain, this was much more like it! Things were looking up.

Three
Hell on Wheels

Abingdon to Osney Bridge, Oxford - Sunday 28th. April

Three weeks later things were definitely looking up. The weather was fine, with a good forecast, David's health was OK, and no-one had eaten Young John's specially selected smokey bacon crisps. Meeting Big John and Ben-the-Dog in Oxford, we had the predictable problem of finding somewhere to park. We would like to thank the aptly-named Payless DIY store on Botley Road who sponsored this trip by unwittingly allowing us to use their carpark all day.

We drove down to Abingdon (where there is never any trouble parking) and started with a pleasant stroll upstream from the bridge over the Rye Farm meadow to Abingdon lock. The fine morning was a welcome contrast to the wind and rain of our arrival in Abingdon earlier in the month, though one drawback of fine weather was immediately obvious - there were an awful lot of people around taking their Sunday constitutional.

There was a boat or two going through Abingdon lock, and I tried for the umpteenth time to explain the why's, wherefore's and workings of a lock to David. I think I succeeded, as he then wanted to know what would happen if both sets of gates were opened at once. It can't be done, I said. "But what if....", says the lad, gleefully imagining great tidal waves of Thames and Thames cruisers sweeping through Abingdon.

We crossed the lock and then stood awhile above the weir, where we watched two canoeists practising their white water skills in the flow from the weir, taking it in turns to get wet and capsize. Young John was due to do some canoeing on his forthcoming junior school outward bound-ish trip to Exmoor, but watching the 'experts' seemed to put him off a bit.

The path was signposted over a large wooden footbridge, which led alongside a ditch parallel with the river. Crossing this bridge we left all the Sunday trippers behind, and were then able to start some serious walking. The path crossed

23

another small bridge leading us along a potentially dangerous track. To the left was a stagnant ditch full of dubious, brown, smelly stuff. On the other side was the Thames itself, barely restrained by an embankment, with the water level a good three feet above our path.

Boldly ignoring the danger, I pointed out to the lads the nearby course of the Abingdon branch railway line, which, though not long gone, had already been dug up and built over. It's a great pity that neither the great Dr. Beeching nor his successors were far-sighted enough to preserve these routes, for these disused railway tracks would have made some wonderful cross-country bridle-ways.

We rounded a large backwater off the river, and then regained our path along the river bank proper. To welcome us visitors to his river bank, a mallard came flying out of the field and threatened to deposit on David. "Hence the name 'duck'", said Young John. The field alongside the river was huge, and filled with a yellow-flowered plant, just starting to come into bloom. This was our first close encounter with the farmer's favourite cash crop, oil-seed rape. Fair enough, it's a glorious yellow colour from a distance, but it's also exceedingly smelly at close range at certain times, and I'm sure the pollen is responsible for a lot of early-season hay fever and asthma. Big John said that farmers were turning more to growing linseed, which, he promised, is a very pretty blue colour. As long as it doesn't make me sneeze or wheeze, I'm not too concerned about what delicate pastel shade it is.

On the opposite bank was a small weir which presumably was the entry to Swift Ditch, the original route of the river. I have to admire the monks of Abingdon who organised the diversion of the Thames's main flow to go much nearer to the town, for it's certainly quite an extra chunk of river they created. Further along on the opposite bank was another small weir which presumably was the entry to Swift Ditch, the original route of the river - or was it the first one, or both? Never mind, it was time for one of Big John's mint imperials. This same bag of sweets had been on all our walks, having travelled the length of the Ridgeway apparently without replenishment. Its age is uncertain, though it does bear a faded label which says, "Have these. I am going outside and may be some time". We made a determined effort at reducing its contents by taking two each.

Maybe it was the rustle of the bag that disturbed two herons. They took off and circled quietly near us. Then Big John made the mistake of thinking 'camera'. One of them departed after the manner of Concorde, and hid itself among crops on the far bank. The other one simply vanished (Beam me up, Scotty?), so we were still without a photograph of one of these grey, gangly collections of feathers.

We left the field of blossoming yellow via a gate set into a thick hedge, and entered an area of former sand and gravel workings which had been partly levelled and returned to nature. The far boundary was formed by the embankment of the Didcot - Oxford railway line, which crossed the river on an iron girder bridge very similar in design to the Appleford bridge so lovingly described on the last walk. As an hors d'oeuvres to this somewhat decrepit construction, there were the rusted remains of a car lying, inverted and unloved, just in front of the bridge. It's hard to say what sort of vehicle it had been in its previous incarnation, but it had disc brakes fitted to all four wheels, something normally only done with up-market cars. It's final resting place was an awful long way from any road - not a very fitting end to what was once someone's pride-and-joy.

The rail bridge itself was brightened by a little graffiti, things like 'Sharon Loves Tony True', and a very artistic but totally unreadable word. There was nothing offensive, but alas, neither was there anything of wit. If we're going to suffer from graffiti artists, it would be nice to have some humour or even an original thought. I've always liked the thoughts of the supermarket waste disposal operator in Evesham, 1973, "Are you trapped in that Bright Moment when you learnt your Doom?".

We passed under the rail bridge, leaving the gravel workings behind to find much improved scenery with proper riverside meadows on our side, and the steep, wooded bank of Nuneham Park on the far side. We talked briefly about having the cash to buy such a large estate for ourselves. David would cut down the trees and sell the wood, then build a huge water slide from top to river. Dreams of untold riches were interrupted by nearby woofing. On the other side of a fence Windsor the dog was a 'good boy, yes a good boy', for barking at us passing strangers, and a 'good boy' for rolling over. Windsor's parents own a big house facing on to the Thames, a Range Rover and another expensive car whose label I couldn't make out. If Windsor the dog had any sense, he'd continue to be 'a good boy'.

25

Nuneham Park's woods gave way to Nuneham Park's lawns. Near the bottom of the lawn there was a dead dinosaur that had had its front legs cut off. David didn't believe me. Young John didn't believe me. I persisted in my opinion that it was a dinosaur. I didn't care if it was the same shape and size as a dead tree. I was firmly convinced that Nuneham Park had a recently-dead dinosaur lying on its lawn. If the estate owners had realised it, they could have made a fortune from gate entrance fees to see it. (And this was in the pre-Jurassic Park days. Think what the interest would be now!) It occurred to me that the pink and posh boat house at the foot of the lawn would be the ideal building for displaying the dinosaur to the public - such a shame they were letting it rot.

A rowing enthusiast, racing himself up and down the river in a scull, warned us of our approach to Radley College boathouse. There were some unoccupied benches at the far end of the landing stage: the nearer ones were occupied by Radley Mums and Radley Dads enjoying a picnic. Attracted by the eloquent vocals emitted by one Mum, I wandered closer to hear what she was saying. Served me right! She was simply enquiring who might like another sandwich. Once again, I'd been fooled by an upper class accent which was making the most mundane enquiry seem like the most profound thought. It must be my peasant upbringing and my inbred respect for the ruling classes that makes me confuse accent with intellect. Actually, I find that those who speak in a posh accent can be just as thick as the rest of us, but with their expensive education and richer vocabulary they can express their lack of knowledge in a much more fluent way.

It really was a beautiful day. There was bright, hazy sunshine, a few cumulus tops breaking through an inversion, and a light, refreshingly cool breeze from the north east. Occasionally this wind strengthened or stopped - a good sign of thermal activity. We borrowed one of the empty benches at the upstream end of the landing stage which gave us a most pleasant view back down the river. I could have happily sat here in the sun all day. Young John took the chance to consult his spotters' guide to the world. He'd seen a couple of Peacock butterflies, some Orange-tips, and a brown Green Fritillary, but we couldn't find anything resembling the black and dangly flying insects which had appeared in occasional swarms.

I was having trouble with my camera which had decided to re-wind itself after just a few shots. After a bit of fiddling I sorted it out, but some of the film has been exposed, and whatever photographic gems were on it have been lost forever.

26

As we set off again, something bright, yellow and dangerous caught my eye. Not more oilseed rape, but David who had stripped off his trousers to expose his violent yellow beach shorts. They are so bright that oil-seed rape pales in comparison, and their glow lit up the scenery for miles around.

The next well-lit mile or so up to Sandford was typical Thames scenery, with meadows either side, occasional bushes and trees, and views of the railway and Kennington to the west and the traffic of the A423 far away to the east. Young John thought he'd seen another kingfisher, but it turned out to be a blue plastic bag in a tree. He did better in spotting two birds, a crow and a kestrel, having a lengthy aerial dispute over some matter, which, after many swoops and twists and turns, the crow appeared to win, as the kestrel dived away for cover.

In the distance was evidence of our approach to Oxford - not the 'dreaming spires', but a view of three of Oxford's four tower blocks. Luckily, these were soon lost to sight as we neared the buildings that had been sited near Sandford lock. Some 'New Age' travellers had also sited themselves near to Sandford Lock, so that we had to pass close by their front doors. I'm in at least two minds about these people - in small groups they are harmless enough, but the bigger group that, for instance, settled on Enstone airfield in North Oxfordshire cost the farmer an estimated £10,000 in lost stock and general damage.

It was time for lunch and Sandford lock was as good a place as any. We had turkey and ham rolls, chicken and bacon pie, and scotch eggs. And..... water-and-whiskey, courtesy of Big John. It was a lovely day for a meal in the fresh air. Young John pointed out a glider flying almost overhead. I watched the pilot feel his way round a thermal, straighten and turn again trying to centralise in the core. After two or three shifts, he found the centre, and circled round and round, gaining noticeably on each orbit.

I also watched the earthbound Sunday strollers around the lock - not one of them saw the glider. However, one chap, although missing the sublime above his head, certainly saw the ridiculous floating on the water. "That must be a fast boat", says the sage, "look at that big white vinyl bench at the back!" He was right. I watched this same boat pass us by earlier, making a lot of noise and wash but very little   progress. It was equipped with enough dials to satisfy any engine freak, including a speedo calibrated to 60 knots, and a depth-measuring sonar device. On the Thames, I ask you! This boat also had one bit which baffled all

27

four of us. The Captain's throne rested on a glass fibre hump the size of a good size footstool. Here's the puzzle. This hump was fitted with a window, the window was curtained, the curtain was drawn tight across. What was it?

Another boat provided us with the lunchtime cabaret. A small two-berth cruiser, which had better remain nameless (Emily) was brought upstream into the open lock. Presumably it was going on up to Oxford. But no, Cap'n Bream turned the boat round to face the way they came. Meanwhile, Britannia was posing out of a forward hatch, though lacking a trident, she had a long boathook in her hand. Were they going to tie up? No, they swept round in another full circle, again ending up pointing downstream. Britannia continued to hold her pose wonderfully, without in any way contributing to Cap'n Bream's manoeuvres. Occasionally they got near to the lock wall - but there was no move to berth the boat. They came to a halt almost in the middle of the lock, Britannia still posing, giving us not the slightest clue of their intentions. Not until we got up to go, some twenty minutes later, did they finally tie the boat up - still in the lock, still facing the way they came.

Rested and refreshed, though baffled, we climbed up past the lock. What did we see? the Kings Arms, that's what we did see, and being full, we did pass it by, only slightly frustrated at missing out. Sandford lock and its surrounds were certainly popular with the local strollers, pubbers and picnickers and there was many a boat moored just upstream of the lock. There were also three all-but-rotted half-submerged hulks which I took to be college barges, long disused. History they may be, but terribly tatty they were. They should either be restored or removed. David, having thankfully felt cold and replaced his jogging trousers over those yellow shorts, was tempted to see how deep the mud was going through a gateway. "Oh!", he said.

Big John allowed us to cut a bend in the path, deviating from the river for a few hundred yards. (This was a rare treat - up to now we had followed the exact line of the Thames as closely as possible.) Finally, we left the tourists behind (for a while, at least), as we neared yet another arched and riveted railway bridge. This one carries the branch line that used to go to Thame and beyond, now only serving Rover's Cowley Works and football hooligans. Crossing another footbridge over the broad Hinksey stream brought us into a short stretch of damp, willow-lined footpath before we reached the 'Gateway to Oxford' - the uninspiring concrete bridge carrying the Oxford Ring Road.

28

A New Age traveller would seem to have given up the travelling life, and had built quite a substantial tarpaulined camp under the bridge, clear of the main footpath. Best of luck, mate - there was a permanent rumble from the traffic passing overhead. The path continued up to Iffley lock, with open fields on our side of the Thames and Iffley village just visible on the other. The lock had a very well-kept garden, and also had a flight of rollers with a neat little see-saw affair for lightweight boats to be pulled by heavyweight owners between the high and low levels of the water, so by-passing the lock. There was also a pub, convenient for those that had worked up a thirst manhandling their craft.

The next mile or so to Oxford city centre was something of a nightmare. Our peaceful Thames Path was suddenly more like a pedestrians M25 and a cyclists M25 all rolled into one. In addition to us four and a dog out for a peaceful ramble, there were tens, possibly hundreds, of locals out for a Sunday stroll. (Many of them had brought their dogs, one of which was most anxious to mate with Ben. Ben has a sensible attitude to gay dogs of doubtful pedigree, and sat firmly upon his tail). There were Oxford cyclists just passing through and keen mountain bike cyclists just racing through. Most dangerous of all were the rowing coaches, wobbling up and down on all manner of bikes ancient and modern, megaphones in hand, yelling encouragement and abuse at their crews who were trying to learn the difficult art of rowing a racing eight. Not only had we picked one of the nicest days of the year so far which had brought all the crowds out, it would also seem that most Oxford colleges had their boats out, training for whatever rowing contest was next.

I never realised there was such an art to rowing. The coach really seems to be superfluous - the bike and megaphone are just toys to keep him amused. It's the cox, seated in the boat and the only one able to see where they're going, who really wields the power. The rudder strings in his hand are just a token of his office, for steering a craft full of eight beefy lads or lasses cannot be done with the minuscule rudder, but requires carefully applied power from one or more of the paddles. The cox demands, and gets, instant, blind obedience from his crew, who seem to be there just to provide the muscle. And for all the high technology applied to boat and paddle design, a rowing eight is not an efficient means of transport. Once under way, even a craft propelled by an experienced crew produces just four horsepower and progresses in a series of stops and starts with the craft all but halting each time the paddles re-enter the water.

I hadn't explored this bit of Oxford before, and the rowing coaches, the crowds and the cycles made our progress anything but a pleasure. It was all shove and bustle, with no chance of a gentle greeting from a fellow walker. Beyond the blue-painted Donnington Bridge the far bank was covered with huge, ornate boathouses, leaving the River Cherwell to wriggle its way into the Thames as best it could. Our bank was plagued with yet more surging, thronging pedestrians and cyclists. This stretch of the Path could be nice: frankly, that day it was a nightmare. Give me peace and quiet on my riverside walk.

On we struggled through the masses, finally reaching Folly Bridge, the nearest we would get to Oxford's centre. The visitor to Oxford would probably miss the access to the Thames from Folly Bridge - there were no signposts, and the access paths to the river from either side looked like they both led to abandoned boat yards. On balance, despite the risk that imaginative signs such as 'Thames Barrier - 125 miles' and 'Thameshead - 50 miles' might well increase the number of people using the riverside, both Big John and I found it disappointing that such a major tourist centre as Oxford has no indication that a long-distance path runs right through its heart (but then, I often feel that Oxford has no heart!)

It was a warm day, weariness was beginning to show, and so, generous that I am, I dumped the lads with Big John, and took a small diversion in search of an ice cream. Sunday trading problems or not, the lady in the shop on the bridge was pleased to sell me four strawberry splits, and as it was a warm day, I had to rush a bit to catch the others up before the lollies melted away. David took this chance to exercise his wit. "No thanks, Dad", he says, as I came pounding up, "I'll save mine till later."

West of Folly Bridge we were instantly clear of the massed hordes. There were still a few locals walking their dogs, but we were getting quite a different view of Oxford from the one the tourists get. We passed under an ornate footbridge, then round the back of the ice rink with its ridiculous external cable supports (I swear I'm going to attack it with my junior hacksaw one day), and under another railway bridge which barely gave me enough headroom.

The path eventually brought us to Osney Island, with the newer Osney Mead industrial estate on our left, and older factory buildings of unknown age and purpose on the opposite bank. We passed Osney lock, where there is an unusually clear map of the immediate area, including all the various waterways around this little piece of Oxford. The final stretch up to the Botley Road bridge is bordered by one of the delightful streets of Osney Town which had some

30

parking spaces on it! So, that's where we should have parked!

And finally we climbed out on to Oxford's Botley Road. Even though it was Sunday, with only light traffic, the noise of car after car was deafening after the (relative!) peace of most of the last ten miles. The final half mile along warm tarmac pavements came hard on our tired feet, made all the harder by knowing that we could have parked so much closer to the Thames.

On reflection, this had been a marvellous day for a walk, especially without the headwind we had last time. Young John was much less tired, David had done well with only occasional grumbles, and my legs were still working, just.

One final thought. On the long two-mile stretch through riverside Oxford, in addition to a total lack of signs, there was not one mobile ice cream and canned drink seller to be seen. I'd had to search for a shop myself. Nothing like discouraging the tourist, is there?

Four
Have an Ice Day

Osney Bridge, Oxford to Northmoor Lock - Sunday 30th. June

The next walk took a bit of planning - it wasn't easy to find a convenient place to finish. There are few road crossings of the Thames upstream of Osney: of those, Swinford toll bridge was too close, even for us, and Newbridge was much too far. Bablock Hythe (what a lovely name!) was the right distance out, but the road route to get there from Oxford is incredibly awkward. We settled on finishing at Northmoor lock, giving us about a 12-mile stroll. All we had to do was find the lock access road.

* * * * *

Just west of the village of Appleton is a tarmac road marked 'Bridleway', pointing in the general direction of the Thames. On a sticky, overcast Sunday morning I turned my car into it, and followed it. Big John followed me in his car. The tarmac became gravel, but I kept on going. After a mile or so the gravel went on to be private driveways, but a muddy bridleway was still marked. Feeling intrepid that day, I got out of the car and explored the muddy bridleway on foot. It was damp, cool and leafy: it was a lovely walk. I found myself going further and further into the dark forest, and getting more and more disorientated. Where it goes to, I don't know to this day, but I do know it doesn't go anywhere near Northmoor lock! I gave up and retraced my steps back in to the daylight. As I got back, I found that Big John had done the sensible thing - he'd gone and spoken to one of the natives in the houses, and got full and proper directions to the real access road to the lock.

We drove back along the mile of gravel and tarmac back to the road, followed the directions, and sure enough there was a sign saying 'Lock Access Only'. Unfortunately it also said 'No Public Right of Way', and to reinforce this, the road was closed off by a locked gate. As I said, I was feeling intrepid that day, so I climbed the gate and took a walk to see if I could see the river. Getting to the crest of a rise opened up a wonderful view over the valley. I supposed the Thames was in the bottom somewhere, though it wasn't visible, and returned up the track. For want of somewhere better to park, we left Big John's car on the verge by the gate.

Though the drive to Oxford took a mere ten minutes, due to my various intrepid deviations it was well past 11.30am. when the three of us (David having wangled a party invitation that he just couldn't miss) and Ben-the-Dog finally climbed up the metal footbridge to the Botley Road, crossed the Thames by the road bridge, and set off went along a narrow muddy footpath.

Though it had been close season for fishing last time out, there was no shortage of serious enthusiastic fishermen now, making up for lost time. The amount of tackle they had amazed us. Armfuls of rods, keep nets, stands for this and that, catapults to distribute ground bait, boxes and boxes of various maggots (how can the fish tell?), and one chap at least must have had thirty or more floats in his special box. Add in brolly, waders, flask and butties, and a big metal box that doubles as a seat complete with extendable stick-it-in-the-water legs, and you can understand why a lot of them also have that big trolley to wheel it all along. I really don't know how many fisherchaps we passed, but they were spaced at about twenty yard intervals for maybe half a mile and more. And what did we see them catch? Three small fishes, which added together might have made a meal for one. That's all that this money, brain and technology had caught.

There are various streams and lengths of water around this area, one of which must have been the connection to the Oxford Canal, though in typical Oxford fashion it was not labelled. We crossed over a metal arched bridge at Medley boat station, passing a slightly shop-soiled cruiser moored up and for sale at 'only' £19,000, then continued along the west bank of the Thames. A sign beckoned us to the Perch at Binsey - we remained unbeckoned. On the opposite bank was Port Meadow, a vast area of flat greenery, and still common grazing land, with a number of ponies allowed free range over it. Our bank was perhaps the more interesting to walk along, being varied in level and dotted with trees and bushes, but both banks are very much in countryside. Although the Thames flows through Oxford, very little of tourist's Oxford could be seen: this was a different world to the colleges and the traffic cock-ups of Oxford. Or nearly - in the far distance, ruining the country atmosphere, stood the vast buildings of Wolvercote Paper Mill.

Young John spotted a heron on the far bank. Big John got the camera ready, but the heron didn't stand out against the background. "Try saying 'camera' ", said I. "Camera", said Young John, and of course, the heron took flight. Craftily

33

though, he landed again before Big John could bring the camera to bear - in the water where he didn't stand out against the background! This heron was fishing for Sunday lunch, and nothing would shift him. We watched a tern have quicker success, picking up something small and wriggling, and also watched a swift, skimming water into its beak as it flew low over the water. That must require some very exacting flying.

A good steady stroll brought us to Godstow lock, and shortly afterwards we passed by the remains of Godstow Priory. The ruins are closed to the public, so we merely said 'very nice' and moved on by. Other things were calling. At the end of this field was a road and a bridge, and a pub. No ordinary pub this, this one was the Trout of Inspector Morse fame. (Inspector Morse is the book and TV. character for whom the geography of Oxford has been re-written. According to the TV. producers, you can, for instance, turn south off Oxford's High Street, travel two hundred yards, and instantly arrive half a mile north at the Radcliffe Infirmary).

It was becoming a warm and muggy day, we were thirsty, and having done a couple of miles already, we deserved a drink. Big John, who was carrying his countryman's heavy waterproof jacket in anticipation of rain, was more than ready for his usual pint of best bitter. Young John had his usual double orange juice. I didn't fancy Guinness. I wanted something long and cool, but not a full pint of alcoholic beverage. Inspiration came to me at the bar - a pint of Strongbow shandy. I don't think I'd ever had a cider shandy before, and it turned out to be a very refreshing drink.

I was disappointed by the lack of excitement at this famous pub. There was not one single TV. star to be seen, and it was a very sombre bunch of Brits that were sat outside, with hardly a smile or a laugh between them. The staff were polite and courteous, but similarly quiet. Did the place only get lively when the film crews were in? Still, we sat enjoying our drinks, listening to the rush of water through the weir, and pondering the purpose of the dis-used and lethal footbridge that still just spans the Thames. (Incidentally, the staff and patrons of this pub have even more reason for gloom now. It suffered a severe fire later in the year though I'm pleased to say that no one was hurt, and that the Trout is still in business).

It was time to get back on the road, and that was easier said than done. The narrow back road past the pub was being used as a 'rat run' by local drivers to avoid the latest road works chaos on the Oxford Ring Road. It took some nifty footwork to avoid the mad motorists before we regained the safety of the fields. Grateful to have survived, we got down to the river bank, and away we went. Well, at least away they went. I'd been drinking cider. This cider had gone rapidly to my legs, and did they feel weak and wobbly! Still, Big John and Young John were going well - I just had to make the effort to keep going. Not far away was the very grey and boring A34 road bridge over the Thames. The queues of traffic which had not managed to by-pass the by-pass were barely moving - even with cider in my legs I was making better progress than they were.

Beyond the bridge was a lovely, easy bit of walking through an open meadow. Though we didn't appreciate it at the time, the grey and boring bridge marks a distinct change in the Thames and its surrounding countryside. The next twenty-five miles up to Lechlade are quite different to the river scene downstream of Oxford. There are no more wide sweeps of river and huge houses with manicured lawns. This is a land of riverside meadows and of solitude. Perhaps the Upper Thames should be called the Isis (or the Sis!). It has such a distinct and different character that it deserves a separate name.

The banks just upstream of the bridge had been very neatly rebuilt. The line had been marked using staked hurdles, then filled in behind, and nature allowed to consolidate it. A vehicle access road took us all the way to Kings Lock, bypassing a few tight loops in the river, and allowing us to overtake a couple of cruisers in the process. We sat at the lock for a while - it felt like time for a short snack.

ATTISHOO! Sorry? ATTISHOO! What? ATTISHOO!-ATTISHOO!-ATTISHOO! Ladies and Gentlemen, it's June, and yes! it's Hay Fever! I thought it was too good to last. Despite having a one-a-day super-strong pill before leaving home, the pollen had won. Perhaps it would subside in a minute. ATTISHOO! ATTISHOO! - no, it looked like I was in for a good attack. Off we went, me sneezing the while. This length of the Thames above Kings lock was really peaceful. ATTISHOO! Lots of meandering bends in the river ATTIS-HOO! bordered by lovely open fields ATTISHOO! full of un-cropped grass, poppies, buttercups and pollen, ATTISHOO! I gave in - in desperation I crunched up one of the two extra anti-histamine tablets I'd brought. Result? ATTISHOO! Young John and Big John strolled on, while I wobbled on under the influence of cider, ATTISHOO!, and drugs that didn't work.

A milesworth of meadows further upstream we passed through a large wicket

35

gate that keeps farm animals out of Wytham Great Wood. This University-owned wood covers the top end of the hill that is the cause of the river's northward loop above Oxford, and stretches right down to the edge of the Thames. The wood was full of assorted hardwoods and also full of undergrowth growing right down to the water edge and forcing us to go single file along a muddy and uneven track. I was of the opinion that the woods were probably full of wildlife. If that was so, Young John wondered, why was there so little to be seen except rabbits? I explained about mad Ben-the-Dogs and Englishmen, especially on what was turning out to be a warm and close day. In any case, all the wildlife would have been at home watching Wimbledon on television. If it wasn't for one thing (ATTISHOO!) I could have really enjoyed this woodland. There were no signs telling us to Go Away so I suggested we come back in the winter for a proper exploration when (ATTISHOO!) my mind would be clear of other distractions.

Little has been said so far of Ben-the-Dog, who is an excellent companion on a long stroll. Unusually for a dog, he wouldn't even chase the rabbits, and trotted happily to heel under voice control, though Big John always used a lead when we were near sheep or cattle. However, Ben-the-Dog does need to be praised. Every time he wriggled though a difficult stile or fence, he turned to Big John and barked, to announce what a clever dog he was for doing it, and could he have a pat please. Mind you, it was a bit much when at one fence Big John and I had to lift him over, and he still had the nerve to bark for being a clever dog.

Soon after leaving the wood by another tall wicket gate, Eynsham lock came into view, with Swinford toll bridge just around the corner. Lunch! There was a handy bench at the lock, and we collapsed onto it, allowing the afternoon sun to warm some of the weariness out of our legs. The weather forecasters had been right - the cloud layer had broken up and it had turned out to be a warm and sunny day with no threat of rain - a lovely day, really. ATTISHOO! All right, it wasn't. Two real walkers passed us, identifiable by their walking boots and rucksacks - the only other real walkers we met along this entire stretch. A typically English formal 'Good day' was exchanged in recognition of us all being members of the Serious Walkers of Great Britain Club.

ATTISHOO! Peace was ruined by a boat passing through the lock, crewed by some of those jolly, bouncy, outgoing Englishmen and their wives that can spoil a contemplative riverside walk. "It's a pound each to watch me", said one. "More if I fall in!". Hay fever makes me very grumpy - what with spoiled peace

36

and ATTISHOO!, I seriously considered a whip-round: I'd have happily parted with a fiver. Luckily the lock was run by the keeper and his helper in a most efficient manner and MV. Cleverdick was dispatched down stream p.d.q. It appeared that the lock-keepers also resented having their peace ruined.

ATTISHOO! ATTISHOO! ATTISH! - half past two - must be time to move on. A brief walk got us to the Swinford toll bridge. Like other bridges on the Thames, Swinford has to cope with weights and volumes of traffic never imagined by its builders. The toll is fixed by Act of Parliament at 2p. a car, and despite the owners' claim that the revenue is not enough to keep the bridge in good repair, they had a recent application to increase the ancient toll fees turned down. Luckily for us walkers they don't have the right to charge for going under the bridge at all - yet! Through watery eyes I took a look at the bridge. We were definitely in Cotswold country: this bridge is built out of limestone, which has mellowed with the years and blends nicely in with the river scenery.

ATTISHOO! We strolled on, at least Big John and Young John strolled on, because I was feeling ATTISHOO! very sorry for myself, and stumbled on peering through a haze of eye-water and sneeze drops. The river is very twisty along this part and we chose to follow a more direct line aiming for the river a little way upstream - as Big John says, we may be keen, but we're not stupid! Well, maybe I was stupid, for with the grass well grown I was disturbing clouds of pollen ATTISHOO! Young John was also beginning to suffer with the sneezes, so I let him have a dose of useless drug too. Even without runny eyes it really was impossible to see the river when we were more than a few yards from the bank, and the only way to keep to the route was to watch for where the boats were apparently sailing across the grass.

There was a boatyard no more than half a mile upstream where we were obliged to leave the riverbank as the footpath had 'crumbled away'. This meant a short stretch of road walking before rejoining the Thames via a cool footpath past some secluded private houses. Away to our left the high grassed embankment of Farmoor reservoir dominated the scenery. In wintertime, the reservoir is home to all manner of water birds, but in summer it's more the haunt of trainee yacht-persons.

The Thames Path, however, swung away from the reservoir to cross the river at Pinkhill lock. We were not tempted by the hand-made pottery on sale, contenting ourselves with playing hopscotch on some stepping stones marking the path through an orchard. We took the recommended but un-signed route which deviated from the riverbank, through a field or two (ATTISHOO!) to regain the Thames a little further on. By this time, the sun was hot, and we were all making very poor progress. The combination of cider, ATTISHOO! and drugs hadn't done me a lot of good - at one stile my legs barely had the strength to lift me over, and I nearly fell down at the far side. Doesn't hay fever make you feel sorry for yourself!

Back by the river, after perhaps a quarter mile, we passed alongside a backwater, which all but surrounds a virtual island a couple of hundred yards across. This was a wildlife paradise with a large part of the water covered with a mass of flowering lilies. Even in this hot part of the day we could hear a variety of birds chirping away in the thick bushes, and a strange, metallic 'chink' repeated at frequent intervals, like a blacksmith tapping his anvil with a light hammer. Only some months later did I find out that this noise was a very grumpy coot complaining about something. He had nothing to complain about here.

Our guidebook told us to leave the river soon after this point, to go to the 'far corner' of the field, and through a 'series of gates'. Off we went, though with not even the vaguest of signposts to point us in the right direction, it was pure guesswork precisely where to aim. Halfway up the first huge field was a gate that looked like it might go somewhere, but it was only one solitary gate, and not in the corner. Ignoring it, on we went up our field (ATTISHOO!), making very stumbly progress through some deeply-ploughed and well-crumbled soil. At the corner of the field was a fence, a thick, scratchy, impenetrable hedge and ditch, but no gate, and no way forward.

Obviously we weren't far from civilisation because we could hear the sound of children's cheery voices not far beyond the hedge, but was there no way of getting through. Whether it was lack of signing, or alterations to hedges and gateways that had brought us to a dead end, we didn't know, but all three of us were getting so fed up and weary that we had to have a sit to get ourselves sorted out. It was already four o'clock, and the heat, the hay fever and the prospect of back-tracking along the ploughing, all still to be followed by several miles of footpath to Northmoor, was a bit too much. Even Big John's water-and-whiskey refresher didn't revive me much, so how he persuaded Young John and me to get going again I'm not sure.

Most unenthusiastically, we accepted the only option and stumbled back along the 400 yards of soft ploughing. I went into head-down mode, simply keeping my eyes on Big John's ancient, well-worn, reddish boots, long-striding steadily in front of me, hoping that Young John was keeping up somewhere to my rear. At the middle of the field, and lacking any other options, we went through the solitary gate. This looked a little more hopeful. We made a diagonal crossing of a grassed field, this one sporting a pair of nice little arched-stone bridges over what might have been a stream once, and reached another gate. We were back on route - there was a proper lane leading away from the gate, just like the guidebook promised.

Three hundred yards down the lane there should be a bridle path. It looked like there could be - there was a lady walking along it holding a bridle, with pony and child attached. "Does this go to Bablock Hythe?". "It certainly does - just follow it till you meet the road", she said, all lightness and joy. She obviously hadn't walked 10 miles in the blazing sun. "Have a nice walk!", she called. How kind of her!

We were back to slogging again. Slog, plod, plod, plod. Horse hooves had made the track very uneven, very hard on tired feet, very niggling (ATTISHOO!) to those with hay fever. And it seemed to go on and on, edging along one side of a cultivated field, with plenty of low-level greenery getting in the way of tired legs. It was hot, sticky, and hard work. Now I know how Chris Bonnington felt trying to climb Everest.

After what seemed like five years (about a mile), the track ended at the promised road. And, perhaps this was the promised land! Look! an ice cream van was approaching down the road! I flagged him down, desperately willing him to stop, ready to throw myself in front of his van if he didn't see me. "Yes, please. What would you like?" (Anything! Everything! Name your price!). I paused for a moment, just savouring one of life little pleasures, baffling the salesman with my slow deliberations. A '99' for Young John, a pineapple split for Big John, and a nice big ice pole for me. Bliss! Magic! it's amazing what the little things in life can mean. If you ever read this, Mr. Whippy, accept our eternal gratitude. Refreshed and renewed, we strolled on. Even the hay fever seemed to be receding.

A few hundred yards of walking along the road brought us to the extensive mobile homes site which all these path deviations were trying to avoid, and by ignoring the 'Private' signs and pretending to be visitors, we finally reached the

Thames again. The name Bablock Hythe was more impressive than the reality. There has been no ferry here for years, and the pub is long-defunct. There was just a car park and a lot of people lying in the sun. There is hope though - the pub is being renovated, with a promise of 'opening soon'. Good luck to them, perhaps they'll even re-open the ferry, and make good use of a secluded piece of the Thames.

We joined the other trippers in resting on the grass. I treated myself to a lie-down, and gosh, didn't my bones ache. I could feel my body regaining its normal length as all the bits were allowed to stretch out. I even took my boots off, making sure I was downwind of the other two. I also kept looking round to see if Mr. Whippy was going to re-appear. Maybe it's as well he didn't - you can't re-live magic moments.

It was already five o'clock, and really was time to get moving. Things were starting to go in our favour - the heat had gone out of the day, the rucksacks were a little lighter - so perhaps we could make the last two miles to Northmoor lock in one go. We were back to the most typical of Thames scenery - meandering banks, short grass, willow trees and the like, and we trudged on, taking advantage of shade where we could. I began to think I could see the white-painted moorings downstream of the lock, but I didn't dare say anything to Young John. The poor lad was flagging badly and I didn't want to get his hopes up in case I was wrong. I also had a nagging fear that the lock might close early, leaving us with no way of crossing the river. But steady plodding succeeded - we did get to the lock. I couldn't believe it. I was sure it was a mirage. Big John got excited for the first time in all the years that I've known him. "It is Northmoor lock", he said. "It is! It is! It is!". The poor chap must have been delirious.

There was no problem about crossing the lock - it was still open with many a boat and fisherman still active. Had we reached this lock earlier in the day, I would have spent more time looking at the removable paddles of the weir. That would have to wait for another day. Young John insisted on two minutes rest before we tackled the road up to the car. I couldn't argue, and gratefully rested my legs one more time.

We just had to complete one last plod along the warm tarmac road up to Appleton. It was narrow and so we had to keep squeezing off the road to let the cars go by. We got to the point where the road climbs the scarp of the 30-mile ridge that runs parallel to the river. This last slope took every bit of strength

40

we'd got. I had trouble finding the energy to will Young John on, and only kept going myself as I could by now see the houses of Appleton in the distance. Shock! horror! even Ben-the-Dog was worn out - just for a moment he came to a complete stop on the hill. Now that was unusual!

One step at a time we scaled killer hill, got onto the flat bit, wriggled through alongside the padlocked gate (if it was padlocked, how did all the cars get through - did they each have a key?) and collapsed into the car. It was 6.00pm. - a planned five-hour stroll had taken six and a half hours of hard slogging, and it was so soul-destroying to be able to drive back to the start point in just ten more minutes.

*　*　*　*　*

Two days afterwards, having recovered from my exhaustion, I flew over the same area in a light aircraft. Knowing the ground intimately, I was able to point out to my passengers the highlights of our walk - and it surprised me how many highlights there were. Perhaps I had enjoyed myself, despite heat and hay fever. Viewed from the air, though, the deviation to avoid the caravan site really did look unnecessary - surely a footpath could be negotiated through it.

Upstream of Radcot. Typical Upper Thames scene on a gorgeous summer's afternoon, with blue skies, still water, pill box and fisherman.

This is where it started - the causeway leading to the Thames at Streatley. As usual, Big John has already taken the lead.

Plate 1

Appleford railway bridge - a collection of chucked cherries held together with iron strips, paint and rust.

Battling mightily against rain and wind, Young John (in his very baggy overtrousers) and the author struggle to reach the relative shelter of Culham lock.

Plate 2

Never mind the 'dreaming spires' - this is the approach to Folly bridge in Oxford's centre which does not inspire.

Swinford toll bridge. Boats at all angles give some idea of just how much the Thames twists and turns in an effort to avoid paying the toll.

Plate 3

'Gentle, farmed, managed, English countryside'
The approach to Northmoor lock.

'Killer Hill' - the access road to Northmoor lock on a beautiful
summer's morn. The Thames is behind the distant trees.

Plate 4

Hart's footbridge, with half of a keen walking family on it, and a lovingly-maintained flower garden drifting through.

Little lost bridge. John and David made a point of walking on it to make it feel wanted. What you can't see is the guardian of the bridge behind the pillar lying in wait for unwary dogs.

Plate 5

Jungle Bashing. Oilseed rape to the left of me, thistles and burdock to the right, John and David overwhelmed by the vicious vegetation.

Tenfoot bridge. Isolated, peaceful. No further comment.

Plate 6

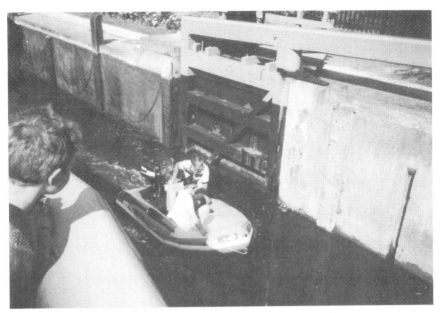

"All that water for one small boat?" Radcot lock.

A V-notched stile, just big enough for a small lad's bum.

Plate 7

*Old Father Thames, ill-clad for the weather, let alone some
serious digging, taking a breather at St.John's lock, Lechlade.*

*Halfpenny Bridge, Lechlade, on a grey autumn morning.
The toll house lights created fantasies in our heads of warmth
and Sunday morning breakfasts.*

Plate 8

*Looking downstream from Water Eaton footbridge, with the
shallow water barely half way up the swans.*

*A young lad in wellies on a foggy December day - the footpath
winding its way towards Ashton Keynes.*

Plate 9

The approach to Lyd Well. This photo was taken in October, after one of the driest summers for years. Six weeks later the water was flowing strongly through the culverts.

"All this way to see a stone?". David, genuinely tired, and John, a little short of puff, rest on the stone marking the source of the Thames at Trewsbury Mead.

Plate 10

Five
Jungle Bashing

Northmoor Lock to Tadpole Bridge - Sunday 4th. August

The day dawned bright and clear, promising "lots of sun and temperatures into the 70's" - ideal if you're not walking anywhere! Big John and Ben-the-Dog joined us more or less on time, and we were off! No we weren't - my sunglasses had disappeared. I frantically ran in circles around the house, but there they were not, so I gave up, deciding to go without. "Last time I saw them they were on David's nose", she said, as I got back into the car. David! both child and shades were sitting like Lords in the front of Big John's car. I retrieved my shades - Big John was welcome to the child.

Knowing the route to Tadpole bridge, I led the way. Not knowing the route, Big John followed closely. Not knowing the route, Big John didn't spot me forget to take a left turn and so add about three miles to the journey. We left Big John's motor by the Trout Inn, anticipating a refreshing pint on our return at "oh, half past two, maybe three o'clock". All five of us crammed into one car for Anne to drive us to Appleton, where we parked alongside the gateway marked "No Public Right of Way. Lock Access Only." leading to Northmoor lock. We posed badly for photographs, discovered that the lads hadn't brought any sweets, and set off on our merry way.

The tarmac lock access road was the same killer hill that almost defeated us at the end of the last walk. With fresh legs, downhill on a beautiful summer's morning, it was a delightful stroll. Being a clear day there was a wonderful view northwards, although the river itself was hidden in the trees along the valley. The insects were really enjoying the summer weekend sunshine. Dragonflies, bright blue damsel flies and butterflies of various shades were all doing their stuff over the wheatfields and on the various flowers in the verge. Little John spotted two damsel flies apparently mating - he found it appropriate that their joined bodies form a heart shape. Big John mentioned a butterfly he'd recently seen but couldn't identify (nor could we from his description), and I remembered days in my youth when we would go hunting with a butterfly net, chasing

42

around like idiots. Attitudes have changed - I wouldn't want to see my two lads chasing, capturing and often damaging or killing butterflies - there just ain't enough to spare. Big John also told us of a picture he once saw, made up entirely of butterfly wings. That's distinctly un-green.

Fifteen minutes leisurely downhill strolling brought us to Northmoor lock, and on this second visit we had both time and energy to look at the system of removable paddles used to regulate the flow over the weir. We crossed the weir to the north bank, and we were off. The weather was just right, what I call a 'big' day, with the fresh clean air of a light northerly airflow giving us a clear cirrus-streaked blue sky of infinite hugeness, and miles of clear views of the country-side. As usual away from the lock there was hardly anyone about, fishermen excepted, and it was very quiet and peaceful.

A goodish mile brought us to Hart's bridge, a simple arched footbridge over the river, and here we took a break. Coming over the bridge were some real walkers! Husband and wife, we guessed, each with a child on their back, one with a parasol attached to the sling to give shade to the younger child. That looked really keen and efficient. This family were walkers after our own hearts. They were equipped for some serious walking, but weren't in so much of a hurry that they hadn't time to appreciate life. They climbed to the centre of the bridge, (a favourite vantage point for the un-hurried traveller), stopped, and let their kids have a good look from the bridge down at the boats - especially the water-borne flower garden that cruised by.

It was time for us to move onwards. I tried to cross the footbridge. Big John pointed out very gently that the presence of a bridge does not impose an obligation to use it. We were to stay on this bank. Bowing to superior knowledge, I set off after the three expert navigators.

Before much longer we could see traffic moving in the distance, and then the twin pubs and bridge at Newbridge came into view. We even meet a few pubbers who had ventured over a quarter mile along the bank. The Rose Revived (or Relieved, according to David) had a garden full of bouncy, happy, noisy, cheerful Sunday drinkers and eaters. We gave it a miss, and chose to cross the ancient and narrow road bridge to the 'Maybush' on the other bank. It was Big John's round, so the lads and me and Ben-the-Dog trooped round to the garden and found a shady spot, sitting propped against a low wall facing the river. Big John arrived with the drinks but Little John was obviously not thirsty, as he threw his on to the grass, and said he could manage without, thankyou. After my problems with cider last time, I tried a lager shandy, and Gosh, it slipped down a treat, cool and not too sweet. David had asked for some pork scratchings. (Now there's a good bit of marketing - 40p for a few ounces of roasted pig skin which would otherwise go to waste). I was unimpressed with this particular brand which had a very strange flavour.

Big John was equally unimpressed by the scratchings, but he was most impressed by the bridge. Newbridge really was new, once, in 1200 and something, and was restored in the 1400's. Some of the stonework looked original, forming pointed arches. This bridge is well able to stand today's traffic, though the masons who built it could never have envisaged that their bridge would easily take the weight of the 32-ton articulated truck that we watched trundle over the arches. Come to think of it, would these masons even have envisaged that such a huge truck would exist? Could they ever have envisaged the gallons of yogurt the truck was carrying, or the thousands of plastic pots that the yogurt was packed into?

It was tempting to stay at Newbridge all day, but we'd completed barely a quarter of the day's walk, so we reluctantly got going. Next to the pub we passed a field full of jolly touring caravans, surrounded by jolly touring caravanners, some sitting in the shade dozing or reading, some playing bat-and-ball games with their kids, one group playing boules in a most unnecessarily boisterous manner. I can't see the point in dragging a caravan to a secluded site in some exceptional countryside, and then sitting there for two days surrounded by other caravans. Perhaps the social life is what they came for - even those dozing in the sun had cheerful, sociable expressions upon their faces.

Leaving the caravans behind the first half-mile or so was through some open meadows, but then the open meadows became overgrown wooded banks. The Ramblers guidebook asked us to try to keep to the footpath 'to help keep it open'. Not us - the overgrown undergrowth needed the attentions of a bulldozer or JCB to clear it - four pairs of boots and four doggy feet weren't going to make any impression on it. So we climbed up the bank and took to an open ploughed field. Obviously others had been this way before as there was a well-trodden footpath along the edge of the field. At the end of the field we dispatched Young John down a very narrow track to the barely-visible Thames, to see if the riverside path was usable. Ten minutes later a scratched, stung and disgruntled child returned to inform us that, on balance, he'd advise against it.

44

So we continued along the edge of the next field, this one planted with wheat, nearly ready to harvest, and cracking noisily as the sun warmed and dried it. Finally, at the end of these fields, a proper pathway took us a short way back down the bank, through a gate and out into a huge open meadow.

Now this is what a Thames walk should be about - not stumbling along the edge of a ploughed field, but sunny summer Sunday stroll along a riverside meadow. And what a meadow this one was! It must have been a good 600 yards long and a fresh green in colour, although a hay crop had already been taken. It was home to just two horses which were grazing way off in the centre of the field. Scattered around the field were a number of horse training jumps, mainly constructed of solid timbers, or occasionally of car tyres. All of these jumps were well made and very well maintained. Somebody must have plenty of money.

Looking at the horses prompted me to ask Big John whether his pair of horses ever get bored, cooped up in their stables most of the time. He reckoned not - horses, he said, are not over-bright, and as long as they have food, shelter, and exercise when they need it, they're quite content. The two horses in this meadow were happy enough with a huge field of grass to go at, and ample room to run around. They were well aware of our presence and, though they continued grazing, they kept a wary eye on us as we got nearer.

We took a break, perching on one of the jumps that also acts as a fence between this meadow and the next. We had found ourselves a wonderful shaded spot under a few trees, the sort of place where a story-book picnic could be held. I took a moment to stop all this walking and just soak up the pleasures of being outside on a lovely day. In this quiet corner of England we were isolated from most of the world, well away from the daily noise and hassle, and this was a moment to be enjoyed. Just as we prepared to go, a young couple walked up and perched in the shade, tactfully choosing a spot some distance further down the fence well away from us. Another pair of serious walkers - this really was a big day.

The following field was nearly as large as the last and we could see still more jumps in the orchard at its far end. However, the footpath left the field via a footbridge, following the river's bends. Young John and David felt sorry for another, dis-used, footbridge that spanned a dried-up drainage ditch, and so they both walked across it to make it feel wanted. Ben-the-Dog tried to take a drink from the water's edge under it but failed to spot the Guardian of the

Bridge, hiding like a troll behind the stonework. A large white hissing swan was not having any dog near his river, and made his point very bluntly. Ben-the-Dog, well acquainted with the aggressive nature of swans, decided he was not thirsty in the least.

I told David that it was about a mile to the next lock, and promised like an idiot that it would be a good place to have a rest and lunch "in about twenty minutes". Walking is not David's favourite pastime, and occasionally I'd lost my temper with him as he lagged and dragged behind time and again. When I was feeling better disposed, like this time, I simply tried to encourage him to keep up with us. As it happened, he had another breather not much further upstream while we watched a river full of canoe paddlers playing what I took to be water tennis. They were having fun, but it looked too energetic for me.

Again the pathway along the river's edge became overgrown, but in leaping athletically up the bank to avoid the bushes we must have entered a time warp. This really was a case of going from the sublime to the ridiculous. One moment we were strolling along an unkempt continuation of a wonderful meadow, the next thing I can remember is finding myself in a nightmare, not so much walking as jungle-bashing - and I hadn't brought a machete with me. The crop on one side of us was oilseed rape, nearly ripe, badly knocked about by the wind, and growing and lying right up to the edge of the field. Oilseed rape is a very tough plant, and this lot was growing a good five feet high - more in places. On the other edge of this non-existent track was a choice of burdock or thistles, also growing five and six feet high, also growing over the path. Put bluntly, there was no path, but put blunter still, there was no alternative.

Jungle-bashing, I said. It's a pretty good description. I found it hard going, so Young John and David must have had one hell of a time. David in particular couldn't see where he was going; the plants were taller than him, and he was continually getting stuck, scratched and stung. In desperation, I got him to put his cagoule on. With that day's temperatures he soon got very sweaty and overheated but at least he was protected from the worst of the scratchy bits.

David's nightmare lasted a good mile - at the speed we were making, that was a good half hour. Long before we finished, the walking couple we left at the fence had caught us up, and asked very politely if they could come by. There really was no room for them unless we squeezed into a gap in the crops - which of course we did. There was just one moment's respite - almost opposite the inaccessible Shifford lock there was a small gap in the burdock, and there sat a fisherman, fishing. For a fisherman he was chatty ("Warm today, innit?"), and he'd made the only decent-sized catch we were to see on the whole 85 miles of our walks. This one fisherman completely filled the break in the vegetation, and there was no room for us to sit. To David's intense disappointment we decided that it made better sense to get all the jungle bashing over and done before stopping for lunch.

The lads took a deep breath and we bashed and scratched on through more tough plant life. 'Nearing Duxford', said the guidebook,'you will hear the sound of the river babbling over the ancient ford'. Hear it we could, but see the river we couldn't. We came to a corner of the field where Big John searched hopefully for a track down to this babbling ford. No track. We wriggled down and across a ditch to look, but there was only a hay-crop opposite, so we unwriggled back across the ditch, and continued around the edge of the rape field as best we could. There, suddenly, the misery ended - there was a piece of part-ploughed rough pasture along our side of the field, and a gate in the distance. I was all for flopping down in the first clear space, but Big John bribed me with a glimpse of his hip flask to get as far as the gate, where we three waited for an exceedingly cheesed-off David to catch us up. Just on the verge of the quiet lane beyond the gate we found a suitably shady spot for a break. Disoriented, suffering from battle fatigue, we collapsed quietly on to the grass.

Recovering somewhat, I realised that Young John had re-appeared - virtually all I'd seen of him since Shifford lock had been an occasional glimpse of his hat through the foliage. (In fact on two occasions that was all I saw - an empty hat with no Young John in it, hanging decoratively on a burdock.) A more important re-appearance was Big John's promised water-and-whiskey mixture which refreshes the parts even Heineken can't reach. Life began to feel a bit better. Oh, no it didn't! David's pork pie had taken on a very flat shape, and it was all my fault of course. I should have carried his lunch for him. Being a dutiful Dad, I swopped pies and let him have my unsquashed one, which he then proceeded to squash and break into pieces so he could get it in his mouth.

By way of a diversion from lunch, David spotted a pair of bugs or beetles mating on a leaf close to him. Their moment of joy was spoilt forever as Ben-the-Dog, attracted by the aroma of squashed pork pies, came over to see David in his friendly doggy way, and sat down squarely upon them.

We perused the map, and tried to decide where we were, having been forced somewhat off track by the recent vicious vegetation. A group of three teenage girls passing by confirmed that the ford was "that way", then dissolved into the usual girlish giggles at the sight of us 'walkers' sitting in the gutter, apparently lost. Weren't they aware that we had walked many arduous miles to get here, steering only by occasional glimpses of the sun through the canopy? Had they no respect for explorers? No, girls, we weren't lost, and to prove it when we got going again we regained the correct path within two hundred yards. So there!

We quickly found the sign directing us to the Thames and ford which showed the route we should have arrived by. We were too knackered to back-track, so we accepted our error and followed the lane past a couple of thatched cottages, and then along a series of tight bends bordered by yet another wheatfield. The sun was working its magic on the wheat producing a wonderfully warm smell. We passed Duxford Farm (with two real dux in a duxpond in the front garden) and not much further on there was another sign promising us a bridleway to the next river footbridge, Tenfoot bridge, 1.5 miles.

We shall remain ever grateful to the farmer, presumably the Duxford farmer, who had taken the trouble to clear the bridleway, cutting a pathway some eight feet wide through his wheatfield. This was another longish field, with the bridleway clearly marked at the far end, taking us around and along some hedging into a second field. The Ramblers' guidebook had promised lots of pointless detours, but the farmer's kindness gave us a direct and easy route. Earlier than we expected, Tenfoot bridge came into view, with a little green lane leading towards it. Little green lane contained a little green frog and little green-minded John carefully captured it for a better look. David wanted to take it home to put in his fish tub, not appreciating the problems of safely transporting a slippy green amphibian fifteen miles on a hot day. "No!", I said, laying down the law as a good parent should, and so, having been properly studied, little green frog was allowed to make his way home.

To celebrate finding the Thames again, we treated ourselves to one more sit in the shade by Tenfoot bridge. A voice made its way loudly over, using the tones commonly employed by young Englishmen embarrassed by unruly dogs. A bounding folloping golden retrieverish lump flopped over the bridge and dribbled over Ben-the-Dog. Its owner came hurrying after it, all apologies to us and abuse to the hound, and attempted to control the dog by attaching a heavy-duty chain to the beast's collar. All this did for him was to ensure that wherever the hound went, he would be sure to follow. The rest of this young party came over the bridge, very subdued and embarrassed by the behaviour of Fido, who had rapidly dragged his apologetic attendant off into the distance. Ben-the-Dog had sensibly retired behind a tree.

From the top of this high, arched footbridge, we could see a green field full of baled hay on the far bank. Back to proper riverside walking, we thought. Wrong! There were two catches. Firstly, access to the field was through thistle, nettle and boggy ditch. Secondly, there was no right of way through the field, and we were asked to 'Please Keep to the Footpath'. Would you believe it - the footpath ran along the only uncultivated piece of land for miles, actually along the top of an embankment specially provided as a tow path in ancient days. Remember, this was the height of the growing season, and the height of the overgrown undergrowth along this little piece of history was a good match for that of the Rape-and-Burdock field. There was no choice but to start jungle-bashing again!

There was one moment of light relief as we got going - the skippers of a pair of boats with 'Porky's Pleasant Picnics' or something written all over them had tied up and were trying to disembark a party of middle-aged picnickers for a riverside picnic. Not being equipped with boots and thornproof clothing, their intrepid scout was having severe difficulty getting across the boggy ditch, and it was obvious that the more mature members of the party had no chance of getting to the field. Anyway, that field had no public right of way! We bashed on, leaving them to hold a committee meeting to decide how they should now re-arrange their ruined repast.

The red and white hats of Big John and Young John again disappeared rapidly into the greenery, leaving David to struggle through as best he could, and me to follow him and, on two occasions, to pick him up when he slipped and threat-ened to give himself an early bath in the Thames. After fifteen minutes hard bashing, I could just see back to Tenfoot bridge through a random gap in the vegetation - we'd only managed four hundred yards!

We struggled onwards, coming after another bashing session to a bit of a clearing with a pill box in it - the first one we'd been able to look at at close quarters. As we expected, it was a gloomy, unloved, rough finished concrete shell, with an apology for an anti-blast entrance. For all its apparent solidity, it really wouldn't have taken much blowing up - one good-sized shell would have dispatched it. Also, as expected, it contained empty beer cans and crisp bags - the most reliable signs of the presence of modern man. Having delved for a moment into the past, we had one more go at the present, diving boldly back into the undergrowth. Our efforts were rewarded - only a few hundred yards onward we found that all good things do come to an end. There was an end to the embankment and an end to the undergrowth, a stile on which to rest (again!) and, joy of joys, someone had taken the trouble to clear the pathway beyond it. Luxury! - we got back to some sensible walking, and even had time to enjoy the river again.

We relaxed and ambled on gently, following the twists and turns of the Thames through some woodlands growing right up to the river's edge. It was nice to be in some cooler air, shaded from the direct heat of the blazing sun. Finally Tadpole Bridge became visible and we mistakenly thought we were home and dry. Surely we were back to civilisation of a sort? - we could see tents, caravans, campers, fisherchaps, even one or two strolling couples, and the Trout Inn. But no, this footpath hadn't finished with us yet - the last two hundred yards of incredibly dense, tangled undergrowth remained uncleared, and feeling tricked and grumpy, we bashed through to the gate leading out to the road.

We very carefully crossed the narrow Tadpole bridge, which is hump-backed and really only wide enough for one vehicle or human at a time. Remember we predicted finishing by "half past two, maybe three o' clock"? Well, it was just after 5.00pm. that four hot, thirsty and exhausted chaps (accompanied by one cool, un-hassled Ben-the-Dog) collapsed onto the counter of an ice cream kiosk in the pub garden. Late as we were, even though it meant risking the wrath of the chefs-who-stayed-behind, we needed our ice creams. We sat in the pub garden violently attacking cones and lollies and cans of cola, and congratulated ourselves on another fine effort. Big John again clicked for the drive home, and we staggered in to find Anne on the phone to Big John's wife Adele, discussing our continued non-arrival, and the proper tortures to be applied to chaps that linger in pubs.

This slight lateness on our part probably had some bearing on the rather sunburnt nature of the barbecue that Adele had prepared for us. Still, it matched the patches of sunburn on our faces where even floppy hats had failed to reach. And anyway, we'd had a hard day, though in fine walking weather, and we were ready to eat anything!

50

Six
One Thing to Beef About

Tadpole Bridge to Lechlade - Sunday 15th. September

Drip, drip, drip. Drip? I sat up in bed with unusual haste. Gosh, it was raining, something rarely seen throughout 1991. The Birmingham Met. Office man on the radio promised that it would clear later. I hoped so. Big John had arranged to join us early so as to leave Wantage at 9.30am. prompt. Being enthusiastic he arrived about 9.10am. which was not a lot of use as I'd just sent the lads out for a bag of mints. However, in his rush to be early Big John had forgotten to bring the map and guide, so he spent most of the time he'd saved phoning home to get the essential details read out to him.

Young John and David returned dead to time at 9.42am, laden with sweeties, and smeared with blackberry juice. We bundled them into cars, and rushed away to Lechlade, parking Big John's motor by St. John's bridge. Arriving back at Tadpole Bridge we found that the car park there was unusually full, and we were greeted (accosted?) by the Landlord who wished to know if we would be there all day - he was fed up with fishermen using the wrong bit of car parking. We reassured him that we were only simple walkers, that Anne would be would be away with the car in a moment, and wasn't it a lovely day? He believed us, and wished us luck. (Personally I felt he had an obligation to be civil to us - we spent over a pound at his kiosk at the end of the last walk! Mind you, hot and thirsty as we then were, we'd have paid any price.)

Did we say lovely day? The Met. Office had been right - the weather had cleared. Bright, hot sun was breaking through as we re-crossed Tadpole Bridge and took the tarmac access road along by the Thames to Rushey lock. The sun's heat was reflecting off the ground onto our faces, more noticeable as the warmth was evaporating the remains of the earlier rain. The rain and heat were also combining to produce some unusual smells - not the fresh, earthy smell that comes from the first rains after a dry spell, more the wet clothing hung-up-to-dry smell, combined with essence of cow dropping. One possible source of the

51

aroma could have been the crop, growing in the field to our right, that we couldn't identify. It wasn't a cereal, it was much too genteel a plant to be oilseed rape, so we took a guess at linseed.

Nearly a mile of this access road brought us to Rushey lock. Like Northmoor, the weir was again of the paddle type, though there wasn't a great deal of water flowing over it despite the rain. The lock-keeper's family were busily engaged gardening. Without exception, all the locks we passed on the Thames were extremely well kept, and this one, with rather more garden area than some, was still a mass of colour even this late in a dry summer. I suppose lock-keepers have the advantage of unrestricted water supplies. We crossed the lock gates and the weir, and once clear of the lock area I tried (and failed) to get an artistically-composed photo of Rushey lock framed by rushes.

We were again back into open meadows bordering the Thames. Away to the north were the group of radio masts at Bampton Castle. Who operates these, or what they are listening for now that the Cold War is over, I don't know. Just a little further up was Brize Norton airfield, and we could hear, and then see, a VC.10 take off and depart, burning lots of tax-payers fuel in the process. Also airborne were the two, evidently elderly, aircraft that flew past us to the south west, just too far away for identification (this means I don't know what they were). They were at quite a low level - I presumed the RAF air traffic controllers at Brize Norton knew of their presence. Having myself piloted aircraft through Brize Norton's control zone a few times, I find their controllers patient and helpful, but very sensitive about us inexperienced private pilots threatening their large expensive transport fleet with our little pride-and-joy's.

I kept promising David that we would be stopping 'at the pub' for a breather, though I didn't tell him how far away it was. David was looking a little flushed and was hanging back and dragging his feet rather more than usual, giving the impression that he really didn't want to walk anywhere that day. I got him to hold my hand, and having accidently steered him through a cow pat or two, he got the hint and put a little more zip into his walking. Cow pats mean cows, and we soon had to negotiate the first of what became a series of cow herds, all feeding by the river. As I've said before, I'm not keen on walking through herds of cattle. I don't care how friendly or timid they can be, three-quarters of a ton of animal should be treated with respect. Lucky for me and my fears, I was distracted from the cows by two more aircraft passing over, maybe Tiger Moths, one of them doing a slow roll just for fun. On a glorious day like this who could blame him?

To the south Faringdon's Folly Hill stood out. This hill was once the site of a castle built in the time of Queen Matilda. Its present name derives from the Folly, a 100-foot prospect tower which was built in the 1930's by Lord Berner, a director of the Great Western Railway who wanted to survey his train set. One of the last prospect towers built in England, the Folly is occasionally open to the public, and its surrounding woodlands are kept as a recreation space. I haven't yet had a chance to climb the folly myself, but I reckon it would be a wonderful view from the top, with the Thames Valley to the north of it, and the Vale of White Horse, the Uffington White Horse itself and the Berkshire Downs to the south.

We passed through another herd of bovines. One of the beasts had a piece of punk nose decoration, a flat plate with spikes pointing forwards. Was it a pedestrian prod, an earth-shoveller or a piece of Ratner's 'jewellery'? - we'll never know. Madame Bovine totally ignored both us and our rude comments on her choice of adornment.

A couple of miles of gentle strolling had brought us to Radcot lock, though it was still a good half mile to the pub. The lads were allowed to help the lock keeper by opening one of the gates for him. They then peered expectantly over the gate, looking for the boat, expecting the QE2, or at least the cross-channel ferry. In the corner of the lock was a little rubber dinghy, fitted with an outboard motor, manned by a crew of two. Personally I should be embarrassed to use a whole lock full of water for a small craft like that!

Further along, on the north bank, was a camp site, with tents and caravans dotted among the trees of a nicely-shaded glade, sited on a sharp bend in the river. It looked to be an excellent spot for a quiet camping holiday. One more field brought us to a footbridge over one of the various streams that take the Thames past Radcot, and this made a good vantage point to see another four bi-planes pass over, all much on the same course as the previous groups. Was I missing an airshow somewhere?

Moored by the river bank was a narrowboat, converted for passenger use, and remarkably similar to the one that I once had the doubtful pleasure of travelling on. Some years back I was among a party of forty-odd that hired such a narrowboat for an evening river trip, which coincidentally left from Radcot Bridge. The brochure was most inviting, offering two hours on the Thames, a bar on the boat, and a basket supper. The price was not unreasonable, so I booked for Anne, the lads and me.

Everything started well, though I'm sure I must have mis-heard mine hostess. I thought I heard her grumble something about people getting muddy feet all over the boat. Off up the river we cruised. It occurred to some passengers that they might be able to enjoy the view more if they opened the side curtains. Efforts to open them were rewarded with a ear-bashing from a very stern hostess asking what they thought they were doing. She then treated us to a long verbal session on leaving things alone, and who did we think we were, but then she supposed if we really wanted to look out we could have just one or two of the many side curtains raised.

Things settled down for a bit, then the basket suppers were brought round. Mine hostess approached me and the lads. John and David, - aged all of six and four - were behaving themselves, quietly kneeling on the seat, peering through a little gap in the side curtain. "Are these children to have supper?", she demanded in her most Headmistressy voice. Little John and David were shocked, not to say frightened, at being addressed like tearaways, and hadn't the courage to answer for themselves. "Yes!", I said, "they are!". "Well," she said, "they'd better sit down, then!"

We got the hint. It was her boat, no one was going to mess her around and kids were most definitely not allowed to enjoy themselves. For the rest of the trip we kept as much gap as possible between her and us as we could in a thirty foot cabin. When we left we said a pointed thankyou only to mine host at the tiller, who seemed blissfully unaware of what went on below deck and who operated the boat single-handed and competently throughout. I tried to sneak a look at his operator's licence to see if the boat really was owned by Fawlty Towers Enterprises.

We walked over the one of the extremely narrow road bridges that cross a total of four branches of the Thames at Radcot. Luckily, traffic is controlled by lights, which gave us a chance to get over in relative safety. Keeping my promise to David, I agreed that it was time for a long, refreshing drink, so we hopped over the wall into the garden of the Swan Hotel. This turned out to be the perfect Sunday pre-lunch drinking place. We had bright, warm sunshine, decent beer, a tidy, green garden, the Thames, of course, and quietly courteous pub staff. To ruin this perfection, one wasp was sent to visit us, so I threw the tray down on the grass, hoping the little terror would be attracted by the spillage on it. I try to be kind to all living creatures, but I don't trust wasps any more than I trust cattle.

Was it time to go already? - getting up from a pub seat gets harder and harder as the years go by. We crossed the road and regained the footpath which now ran along the north bank and took us through more open riverside meadows. I managed to capture the typical Upper Thames scene on film - it shows a meandering river, the very flat water reflecting a blue sky dotted with steets of fair-weather cumulus, sun-browned rough pasture on either bank, a pillbox, and the power lines that have followed the river's course from Oxford. The meandering and the slow flow were a bit surprising - I was always taught that near its source a river is fast-flowing and runs straight. The mile or so above Radcot must be some of the most isolated and peaceful bits we came across - just us and the countryside on a blue, late summer's day. Whenever I think back to the walks we did, this is my favourite spot - beautiful, isolated, English countryside.

Quicker than we anticipated, we reached the next lock at Grafton and thought we'd found ourselves a quiet place for lunch. Well, we thought we had. It wasn't exactly noisy, but there were several boats waiting to go through the lock, and as it appeared to be the lock keeper's lunch hour, the lock was being operated by committee. Things, of course, did not run smoothly enough for the self-appointed experts among the boatmen, and there were a few exasperated grunts and raised eyebrows at 'some people' who were not conversant with the etiquette of opening and closing lock gates and sluices.

We also made the unfortunate error of sitting very close to the water point. It seemed like a good idea at the time, allowing Ben-the-Dog get a drink, and us to top up our water bottles. There was also a hose, which I took to be a fire hose, but turned out to be for boats to re-fill their tanks. A large cruiser tied up right by us, crewed by a couple who had already waved a friendly good morning to us earlier downstream. Mrs. Cruiserboat leapt off to re-fill the tank, pulling out the hose. The hose had a narrow metal pipe at its business end; even so it barely fitted into their boat's filler hole. So when she turned the water on, of course the hose shot upwards out of the hole, soaking Ben-the-Dog, spraying Young John, and embarrassing Mrs. Cruiserboat. Mr. Cruiserboat rose to the occasion. "Can't get the staff these days, can you?" But then they baffled us by carefully wiping the spillage of good, clean tapwater off their boat. I always thought boats were designed to withstand a little wetness.

While Young John dried himself, I consoled myself on his misfortune with a nip of water-and-whiskey. Big John had lately been genuinely surprised when I gave him a bottle of Bell's whiskey saying to him I felt I really ought to make a contribution. What I didn't say was the bottle had been a gift to me, and I really don't like the flavour of Bell's. Well diluted with water, though, I can stand it!

It was time to move on. The walk continued to be through very pleasant meadows, though there was a distinct whiff of cow dollops in the air. With this sort of easy-going countryside, we tended to walk each at our own pace, first one then another taking the lead, and one or other of us bigger chaps getting ahead or dropping back to take a photo. We took more and more photographs as we went upstream. I think this was not only that the scenery justified it, but that both Big John and me realised, as time went on, that this walk was becoming special to us, and we wanted to keep a record of it.

Young John spotted a heron. We badly wanted a photograph of a heron. Big John fumbled for the camera, but too late! the heron had sneaked out of camera range before he could catch it. This was to be the last time we saw heron on the Thames. Each time we saw one we tried to get a photograph. Each time we'd swear that the heron concerned knew we were trying to capture it on film, and deliberately flew either out of range or to a point where it couldn't be seen against the background. Believe me though, there are plenty of herons to be seen, or perhaps there's just one heron with a warped sense of humour that spends its non-fishing time teasing tourists.

Our path continued to meander. We passed through a number of conservancy gates, but the numbering system apparent at Streatley had long disappeared, and the woodwork was often badly in need of repair and paint.

The path took us finally through a long field which had another huge herd of bovines in one corner. I hoped and hoped that the path kept away from them, but I didn't hope hard enough, and we were forced closer and closer to them. It was milking time and all the good little cows were queueing up by the gate ready for the farmer to relieve them of their load. Personally, I'd have been quite happy to forego my day's milk ration if it meant that all this beef hadn't clustered around the same gate that we had to use. We tippy-toed very tactfully, very quietly through, trying to keep Ben-the-Dog hidden among our legs. Just as we left, an enthusiast came the other way on his mountain bike. He was obviously a farmer's boy - he rode straight through the herd, cattle scattering in all directions. I admired his strength and courage. Ben-the-Dog, incidentally, doesn't admire cattle grids. He can tell you from painful experience that they are totally dog-proof as well.

We paused by a large sign inviting us to the Plough at Kelmscott, but being a bit too late for the lunchtime session we declined their kind offer - and it would have meant extra mileage there and back. We kept on following the Thames and after a short spell weaving through some bushes, we found ourselves flanked by a large field of sweetcorn, growing high in the best cornflakes tradition. David viewed this high greenery very suspiciously, having painful memories of thistles, burdock and oil-seed rape, but the path here remained open and perfectly walkable.

Across the river we could see Eaton Hastings church, looking very lonely by itself, being isolated from such village as there is. The far bank was a sort of lay-by for boats - there were lots and lots of of water-borne tourists, and lots and lots of noisy children threatening to fall off boats into the water. Eaton Hastings had a flash weir and a pub once - all that remains to mark the spot now is a footbridge that we didn't need.

We crossed the river further upstream by means of a generous concrete farm bridge brought us to Buscot lock. Like Eaton Hastings, this was a favourite spot for tourists. The late summer sun had brought them out in droves by boat and even by foot. A number of fishermen were also making their way home from the river via the lock, trundling their equipment trollies, and struggling with oversize bags stuffed full of rods. It's a good job there are no overseas venues for fishing contests - these chaps would never be able to get all their gear on an airliner restricted to 'one suitcase and one small piece of hand luggage'.

Peering optimistically into the distance, I could see the tall spire of Lechlade church about a mile away. The car, then, parked at St. John's bridge, could be no more than half a mile away and I decided that I'd got the strength to get there in one go.

The last long field had an electric fence around it, annoyingly confining us walkers to the river bank. The river flows around the field in a huge loop and it was tempting to take a more direct route. Both Big John and me looked at the number of people who were successfully crossing the field without any irate landowner shouting or shooting at them, so we gave in to temptation, ducked

57

under the fence and slipped across the field too. By doing this, we cut off a good quarter mile of leg-work (the Thames always in sight, so we weren't cheating), then we nipped back under the fence again. In bending down my back touched the fence, my knee touched the ground, and Wallop! I remembered how nasty an electric fence can be. A little further along the bank was another possible cut across the same field under the same fence. No way!

Although we could now see Big John's car parked on the far bank, we had to deviate from the river and follow a track and road for the last quarter mile. Since our walk, plans have been made to provide an additional footbridge to avoid this detour. Unfortunately, the Architects have been allowed to design it, and have made proposals for a carbon-fibre construction! No! I say - all it needs is a nice simple arch in traditional materials.

The final stile out of the meadows was a design I hadn't seen before, with a narrow V-shaped notch for humans to use. David, having less energy than the rest of us, found it an ideal size for a small lad's bum. The track took us along a lovely, leafy, dappled-sunlight lane, a refreshing change from being in the bright sun all the time, and then a couple of hundred yards of back roads brought us to St. John's bridge and Big John's car. (Coincidence? The pub here is also called the Trout, like the pubs at Tadpole Bridge and Godstow). We'd made good time, and would be early for tea for once.

This had been the nicest of all the walks we'd done so far, ideal weather, level walking with the path by the river the whole way, no hassles (apart from the cows) and not too many miles. Lechlade is the navigable limit of the Thames, and hence the end of the towpath, such as it was. I doubted that the remaining lengths would be so easy.

Seven
Grey Start - Golden Finish

Lechlade to Cricklade - Sunday 13th. October

Nothing like being organised is there? No pies, no tasty sandwich fillings - I'd almost forgotten that Big John and me had arranged this date. Saturday night's forecast had promised 'mist, clearing early, some sun and some showers' - a peep out of the window on Sunday revealed a grey misty morning and dew on the lawn. Dew? that meant wet feet for David unless... So with yards of black carpet tape, I tried to patch all the airholes in his trendy white boots. It was worth a try, but I had my doubts. So did someone else, so following a belt-and-braces directive from she-who-knows-best, I also packed spare socks and a towel for the lads.

Cricklade is a good forty-minute drive from Wantage, and being strangers to the town, we anticipated difficulties in finding the Thames and in parking. No problem - there was a huge sign saying 'River Thames' conveniently placed at the bottom of the main street, and there was plenty of room to park Big John's car alongside the river. 'River' was actually a bit of an exaggeration, even 'stream' would have been a bit generous - in fact the huge sign, laid horizontally, would have been nearly large enough to act as a footbridge over this tiny trickle of a Thames.

There is no direct route from Cricklade back to Lechlade, but it was great fun taking the back roads via hidden villages like Meysey Hampton, Meysey Marston and Little Lambsey Disey. We pulled up just on the Oxfordshire side of St. John's bridge at Lechlade and, leaving the car pointing in the right direction for Anne to drive it back home, we strolled into Gloucestershire and down to St. John's lock, the highest lock on the Thames. In the lock garden reclined a carving of Old Father Thames, moved here from the source some time ago to keep him from being vandalised. Not only was he very skimpily dressed for such a chilly morning, but even under the lock keeper's protection he looked old and worn out - I knew how he felt.

59

Our first half mile was through open riverside meadow, used by tourists in the summer, and infested with fisherpersons in October. On a grey, wet day lots of grey wet chaps (trainee Prime Ministers maybe?) were doing their stuff, which is more than the fish were doing. Several of the anglers had black rods of an immense length, perhaps 20 feet long. Presumably they don't cast out with something like that - just hit the fish on the head with the heavy end, or spear them with the pointed end.

St.John's lock was lost to sight in the mist well before we reached Halfpenny Bridge, where the main Swindon road crosses the Thames. It was built in the 18th. Century, and like many old bridges, is too narrow for today's traffic, so it's equipped with traffic lights. The footpath passed under a low archway on the south bank, while on the north bank there was the old toll house, part of the bridge structure and still in use as a dwelling. My imagination played a trick on me here. The lights were on in the tollhouse, rectangles of warmth and comfort in the Sunday-morning gloom, and I could imagine the occupants lazing around, drinking tea, reading the papers, and most importantly, cooking some bacon for a late breakfast, enjoying its mouth-watering aroma. Jealous? Me?

Arriving at a stile not far beyond the bridge, Young John claimed he was in desperate need of first aid. His boots were already damp, and his socks were rubbing on his eczema. Few things in life are more fun than rendering first aid to a child's foot in a muddy field on a damp and grey Sunday morn - and we only had a choice of Wasp-eze, plasters and Savlon to repair him with. Wasp-eze didn't seem appropriate, so I used generous quantities of the other two, told him it would be all right 'soon', and sent him on his way. At the next muddy gateway, another small child was in trouble - at the tender age of 2-and-a-bit she was in grave danger of stepping out of her little red wellies which she proclaimed loudly to her Mum had become 'STUCK!'. We really owe her Mum an apology, because if we'd been gentlemen we would have either helped to retrieve the child, or held Mum's pushchair and dog for her while she slithered in the mud after the kiddie. Sorry, Missus - we were concentrating so hard on our task that we really weren't thinking.

Ahead of us was a large, round, creeper-covered building, which was originally the lock-keeper's house sited where the former Thames and Severn canal joined the Thames. There was no sign of a canal now, except the remains of the bridge footings on our side of the river. Deceptively, the round house was on the far bank, so we had to admire it from a distance. Following the river round brought us to the end of a field, and to a metal footbridge constructed like a set of parallel bars, and requiring some very difficult contortions to get off the far end with dry feet. We then optimistically tried to follow the line of the river, but it couldn't be done. Nearing the village of Inglesham at the corner of the next field all we found was an impenetrable hedge, and private gardens beyond. The Thames Path is incomplete, and Lechlade to Cricklade is one of its most incomplete stretches. After little more than a mile of Thames-side strolling, we were obliged to cross a field, go out onto a lane, and then proceed to walk alongside the noisy, busy A361.

It could have been worse - there was at least a reasonable width of grass verge to walk on for most of the way. The traffic was quite light, but whipped by frighteningly fast. There was evidence here and there of collisions - door mirrors, wheel trims - and David found evidence of what an untidy species we are - cola cans, beer cans, crisp bags - all presumably discarded by passing motorists, as no sane person would choose to walk along this verge. David also discovered several MacDonalds wrappers, and was quite prepared to walk the twelve miles to Swindon if he could visit them for lunch.

Rounding a slight curve we found an obvious gap in the hedgerow where something had gone off the road, sadly marked by what has become an all too familiar sight along today's roads - bunches of flowers in memory of 'Neal and Paul'. The bunches were fresh, with simple messages from the relatives. What else was there to do but stand a moment and reflect on another two lives wasted on the roads? We walked on, rather subdued for a spell.

Young John found a safe place for a rest, and David suggested I might look at his feet. My carpet tape had worked wonders on his boots, holding in all the water that had soaked in through the material. One foot at a time I dried his feet, emptied his boots, squeezed the worst of the water out of his socks, and told him his feet would be all right 'soon'. Young John took the chance to change his socks for his dry pair, and tied his wet pair on to the straps of his rucksack to dry, little soggy flags flapping gaily in the breeze.

A further half mile or so brought us to the point where we could leave this road. It was marked with a sign saying 'Restaurant' which made David happy. I ruined his happiness by saying "No". In any case, the restaurant turned out to be either closed or closed down, which saved me any further argument. Our guidebook told us to next take the bridleway alongside a house that sells goat's milk. This

61

was easy to spot - it was exactly opposite a goat which was tethered to a large concrete-filled wheel. David likes goats, even the pair he met in his younger days that tried to eat his coat. Discussing goats led on to discussing guinea pigs 'like the one at school' and how he'd like to have one so he could 'pick it up'. Kids and pets are incompatible. Pets get discarded after two or three weeks, and mugs like me end up looking after them. I know - I did it when I was young.

All this gabbling about pets distracted me from navigating. We should have been following a bridleway along the edge of a field, but a hedge marking the way had been partly grubbed up, hence we were a little uncertain where the exact track was. Matters were not helped by electric fences and beef on the hoof that were barring the way. Peering around large gaps in the remains of the hedge revealed no alternative to using the same field as the cattle, and worse, the farmer had kindly provided his fence with a lifting handle, and signs inviting us to use it for access. (Why didn't he put another sign simply inviting us to get trampled and gored by his beasts?) We sidled very quietly towards the bovine masses and suddenly! another gap in the hedge meant we could sneak past them, then regain the proper track further down the field. That fooled them! As we slipped back through the hedge we just had time to unhook and re-hook the far fence before the baffled bovine beasties realised they'd been diddled and deprived of their game of Intimidate the Walker.

Approaching a copse I could see a caravan parked among the trees, but as we followed an obvious track around and over ditch and footbridge, the caravan vanished into thin air - I couldn't see it at all. That struck me as odd - the copse was not that thick with trees, so the caravan could only have been a few yards away - unless it was not a caravan at all, but Dr. Who having finally got his TARDIS fixed.

The next mile and a bit of the bridleway wasn't bad walking. Provided we forgot that this was supposed to be a walk along the Thames and pretended we were simply going for a ramble, this was a very agreeable piece of countryside. Even the sun broke through the gloom. Young John had managed to find some burrs which were very attached to him, and proved very difficult to dislodge. The pleasure was also spoilt rather by an electric fence whose white plastic supports were leaning way over the footpath, leaving us very little safe walking space. It was very tempting to break the Country Code and walk on the man's crops, especially when Young John, distracted by dislodging burrs, lost his footing and got a shock from the fence.

The bridleway finally rejoined a road, and a short distance took us back towards the Thames. We bypassed the stile which was the access to the to the next bit of the path, and walked another fifty yards to Hannington Bridge to take lunch. By squeezing well into the verge, there was room enough to sit and admire the river - or what was left of it. Old Father Thames had really reduced in size since Lechlade, and though a couple of fisherchaps were making a brave go of it, there was not a lot of width or water by this point.

For mid-October the mid-day weather was pleasantly mild, and it was warm enough to sit and enjoy a brief picnic. It was made even more enjoyable by a nip of water-and-whiskey. Of course, there was a catch, and I got the thrill of helping David to change his socks. Big John looked on, all concern and understanding, but wisely not offering to help. Like I'd done on more than one previous occasion, I found myself asking Big John if he ever wished he'd had children. "No", he said, smiling.

I couldn't face the thought of both children strolling along with their soggy socks flapping in the breeze. So, taking a deep breath, I bolted down the tasteless cheese roll I'd brought for my lunch, thus emptying a plastic sandwich bag to hold David's aromatic cast-offs. The things we Dads do!

Even with a warming tot inside me I was starting to get a bit chilly and stiff. Three keen people and one dog leapt up to go, and I creaked to my feet, stiff in both legs and hips. We retraced our steps fifty yards or so to the stile where Young John suddenly stumbled and then flashed me a look of sheer terror. He was right, I did ask him if he 'enjoyed the trip'!

Once over the stile, the path ran parallel with the Thames, though some way from it. The first field led to a second by means of what the Ramblers book described as a 'simple plank footbridge' - a grand name for a tatty piece of thin timber perched precariously across a deep, nasty, prickly little ditch, followed by a tricky scramble up into a large field of cows. I was very pleased to skirt round the edge of the field, as requested, to keep well away from the cattle. A cow-proof (and at my advanced age, nearly human-proof) wooden footbridge took us into a third field which had been ploughed, with a track newly-levelled across it. This track finally led us to the orchards and hen-houses next to the house at Blackford Farm (very tolerant of them), and then out of a gate to follow a winding country lane.

Over the river was the village of Kempsford, and also visible was a radio mast, part of RAF Fairford, which had recently been mothballed as an active station. Fairford is the site of the bienniel International Air Tattoo, which I've been to on several occasions. In 1991 I gave it a deliberate miss. The organisers had invited to the show 'in recognition of their efforts' the USAAF B-52 bombers and their crews that had operated from here during the Gulf war. I had a double objection. Firstly, I had suffered the personal inconvenience of being woken up on several mornings by these brave lads flying over my house on their way back in to Fairford after their raids. Secondly, and much more fundamentally, I saw no reason at all to celebrate dumping ton after ton of high explosive from a great height onto, for the most part, innocent victims of Saddam Hussein's ambitions. That was no cause for celebration, only for sorrow.

We were somewhat surprised to find a coach depot along this little lane - we really thought we were miles from anywhere. A couple of the coaches were preparing to move off, and I raised with Big John the correctness of thumbing a lift, since we were merely walking a road. OK, he said, but just as I got my thumb ready Big John, purist that he is, added that we'd have to return to walk the stretch on another occasion!

At the end of the lane we followed the roads through the small, peaceful village of Castle Eaton. Young John wanted to know if it was originally called Castle Eaten, as he couldn't see any sign of a castle. We took a chance on a slight detour which promised to bring us in viewing distance of the Thames. Lucky we did, because this detour also brought us in viewing distance of the Red Lion. It was still open, and quick calculations told us we'd have time to walk off the effects of any drink before driving again. Conscious of my muddy boots and muddy trousers, I drifted in to the carpeted bar while Mine Host's back was turned, and stood very close to the counter where I thought he could only see the top half of me. Initially when he turned round he called me 'Sir', but something obviously caught his eye, as he forgot to give me my change until I'd got both hands full of brimming glasses - very subtle.

Catastrophe! - there was a sign on the garden gate saying 'No Dogs'. Ben-the-Dog never learnt to read, so he was a little baffled as to why we stood round in the carpark to drink and rest. Small, white-and-black terrier-sort-of Fido appeared. We assumed Fido was the pub's dog - certainly he didn't think that the 'No Dogs' ruling applied to him, or perhaps he hadn't learnt to read either.

But, like many a pub dog, Fido had learnt how to make total fools of the customers, and brought us a selection of thin twigs to play Fetch. Like total fools, we fell for it. Fido was friendly but daft, chasing only selected twigs, and then shaking them and chewing them into shorter lengths before dropping the soggy remains for us to throw again. Proof of Fido's ownership came when a door opened and the word 'dinner' was heard. A white-and-black streak departed, leaving clouds of paw smoke and a blue haze of ionized air.

A further 20-yard detour to the Thames itself just to the rear of the pub showed that the river, while remaining a delightful sight, continued to diminish to no more than a stream. Castle Eaton bridge, massively constructed of green-painted riveted iron plates, was excessively generous for a quiet lane over a such a titchy watercourse. It was apparent from a glance upstream that it will be a long while before the Thames Path becomes continuous, as all we could see were a series of much-loved gardens backing on to the river.

We were obliged to take to the roads again, following the the long boring road walk as advertised in the guidebook. It's a good job the weather had improved, with some hazy sunshine beginning to win through, because there was little else to recommend this road. We occasionally had to squeeze onto the verge and wait a few moments to allow traffic to pass, but even these enforced pauses were little respite from a more-than-a-mile-long road plod.

Taking the lead again, as often was the case on the more tedious bits, Big John found us a gateway with a five-bar gate on which to rest our weary bodies. Perhaps this road was not so bad after all- it was nice to lean on a gate on a bright autumn afternoon looking into a field. The land and soil were very different from the downland around Wantage, definitely river valley and much more like the Vale of Evesham of my youth. The tower of Cricklade's church was standing out against the background haze, perhaps two miles away as the rook flies. With the end of the day's walk in sight, it was nice to again be able to relax a bit and contemplate the peace of the countryside.

The peace of the countryside was marred by some inconsiderate gardener using a motor-driven lawnmower, polluting the autumn silence. For a minute or two the noise stopped, and exactly at the moment when we thought that his day's work was done, the wretched gardener started up again. Noise or not, though, David would have sat here all day given a chance, so I compromised and allowed him exactly three more minutes before dragging him to his feet and persuading

65

him to plod on.

In the distance there was a farm which we kidded ourselves marked the point at which we could get off this road. Wrong! OK, then in the far distance was another farm which we kidded ourselves marked the point at which we get off this road. Right! And, for the second time in his life, Big John got excited and raised his voice ever-so-slightly to celebrate reaching his goal.

The farmer had a very helpful attitude to walkers. Opposite a large and noisy rookery (Rooks For Hire - Distances Flown), a large sign saying 'FOOTPATH' pointed us away from his driveway, and a second 'FOOTPATH' sign pointed us through an incredibly muddy gateway and along a clearly-visible farm track. This farmer was also a witty sort of chap. His third 'FOOTPATH' sign pointed us through a gate directly into the side of Buttercup the cow, who had strolled over to be first in the queue for milking. Buttercup and her companions had done what cows often do, and done lots of it, carefully trodden it into the mud, and then stood back a little to watch the spectacle of four humans, fitted with two-wheel drive only, struggling to make any headway. Slipping by as carefully and quietly as we could, we went through a series of gates to arrive in a slightly less muddy field and, joy of joys, there was the good old River Thames coming into view.

Water Eaton footbridge took us over a trickle of water that masqueraded as the Thames. Access to the bridge was tricky for one of my advancing years with what felt like a yard-high step up. It was worth the climb, though - the view from the bridge was lovely. The cloud was now well broken, and with the sun getting lower we were blessed with a perfect autumn afternoon. We took time to watch a few swans in the river. I told Young John that the water was really shallow here - look, I said, it only comes half way up those swans.

Just upstream of the bridge the River Ray joined the Thames, and once past this point the flow of the Thames itself became minimal. In places there was complete weed and algae cover across the river. In the distance were two young lovers out for a Sunday walk, and for the first time in this entire adventure, we caught up and overtook someone. I expect that they're still out there now, making their very leisurely way along the bank. I couldn't blame them - this was a little gem of a spot, intensely green, all banks and hollows, dappled with autumn afternoon sunlight and shadows.

Another half mile brought us to Eysey footbridge, the last footbridge of the day, and into another field of beef. Most of them left us alone, but both the beef and us were trying to use the same bit of riverbank. One of the young bullocks finally took exception to Ben-the-Dog trying to sneak through his field, and came bounding and bouncing up towards Big John, Ben-the-Dog and me, retreated and then came bounding and bucking up again. "Steady!", I said, in a big deep voice. I don't know who was more surprised, me or the bullock, because it worked! - the frightened bullock sheered off and ran away, and we were left to stroll on without further threats, me feeling heroic and amazed. At the end of the field we squeezed gratefully through an iron V-notched stile, leaving the bouncy bullock far away.

Beyond the stile, David, as was often the case, was lagging behind a little, but this time I could hear a gleeful voice saying, "that's good...that's not set...a bit crusty". On turning round I found that the little darling had taken to cow-pat testing for some obscure reason all his own, carefully treading on each one to test its hardness. "David, dear", I said, "you realise you will have to clean your own boots". "Ah!", he said.

One further stile and we were nearly there. The concrete monstrosity of the bridge carrying the main A419 over the Thames loomed up, yet this concrete monstrosity provided the day's magic moment. Direct sunlight doesn't penetrate under the bridge, and without sunlight there was no weed and no algae, just clear water and a clear view of the river bed. Better still was a clear view of a number of large fish. Young John, of course, had brought his spotter's guide with him, and identified the nearest fishes as two young pike, each about a foot long, lurking around, sizing each other up as a meal. We stood and watched this battle of wills, leaning on the galvanised safety rail, interrupted only by a vivid streak of blue zapping across the water - a kingfisher! Now that lot was worth walking all this way for.

But magic moments or not, we had to go. We had a tea promised. One last acre of mud and (to David's delight) cowmuck brought us to a stone stile, then Big John and Young John kindly took a wrong turn to allow me and David to get ahead for once. A short walk through Cricklade, and there was the car, all comfort and welcome. Big John reckoned we had already achieved a great deal in walking all the way from Goring and now that we had completed so much, we were actually looking forward to exploring the final miles.

67

Eight
The Black Hole - and Beyond

Cricklade to the Source - Sunday 1st. December

We nearly didn't get to explore the final miles. In thick fog, with visibility of barely 100 yards, we were driving quietly out to Cricklade following a truck that was following a learner driver, all three of us going steadily in the very marginal conditions. Whoosh! up came the health hazard - a bright shiny red Cavalier which whipped by us on a blind bend. The Cavalier driver rapidly got bored and simply overtook the truck regardless of road or fog. He was then stuck behind the learner, and tailgated the poor novice for a short distance, before zipping past in a third, equally daft move. Big John and I seriously wondered whether he was drunk, or alternatively, as I explained to the lads, he was fitted with radar. A simple operation, I said - open the skull, remove the brain, and a radar set fits nicely in the remaining space.

The rest of the run to Cricklade was thankfully uneventful, and we parked in the handy lane right by the Thames. The River Thames was very different to our last visit six weeks previously. November's rain had turned it into a very vigorous stream. We crossed by the road bridge, and, as directed by our guidebook, took a footpath which led across a series of fields, vaguely parallel to the line of the Thames. The grass was wet, the fields were waterlogged in parts, and I was glad the I'd had the foresight to put Young John and David in wellies. I wasn't wearing wellies, though. My boots had been dosed with dollop after dollop of 'Race', a 100% natural waterproofing for leather. This product has been developed and produced by Claire Whiston, a long-time friend of Big John and his wife, and I'd had a jar as a free sample. (This is the nearest we got to any sponsorship, and this is the nearest Claire's going to get to any free advertising.) I was putting complete faith in Claire's assurance that 'it really does work'.

The footpath, having wandered across this series of fields known as the North Meadow Nature Reserve, rejoined the river bank for a short while, facing us with the problem of crossing the River Churn where it joins the Thames. Though the Churn is a stream rather than a full river, it was several feet deep,

68

and quite fast flowing. Never mind, there was a footbridge - or there used to be. Only one substantial piece remained - a baulk of timber, perhaps 10" x 2", placed edgeways, was still firmly spanning the stream. For the other foot, however, there was only a loose piece of 3" x 2", long enough to reach across, but very springy. Luckily at the bottom of its sag it rested on the remains of a post in the stream bed.

Being the only non-swimmer, I was volunteered to go first, using one piece of timber for each foot. Step-bounce, step-bounce, I got across without falling in. Young John followed cautiously, then David followed very, very cautiously. Big John had no problem, but what about Ben-the-Dog? If he had been properly trained as all the best police dogs are, he would have coped easily with two parallel beams spaced nicely for his doggy paws. However, Big John had neglected to teach him this valuable trick, and the poor old dog was baffled. So Big John walked a little way up the Churn to find a slightly narrower part, then encouraged Ben to jump. If only the stream had been narrower still, Ben-the-Dog would have made it. Did I laugh? No - I refused even to smile at Ben-the-Dog's discomfort, because I knew what was coming. Before long we reached a hedge which was negotiable only by the first Ben-resistant stile of the day, and soggy doggy or not, we had to lift this still-dripping beast over.

Out of the fog loomed another potential hazard - the first field of cows, though this herd was peacefully grazing at the limits of visibility, and didn't appear to notice us. Surprisingly, the thick fog added to our enjoyment of the morning. There was no wind, so it was pleasantly mild, but we could see barely 100 yards, and more than once were disorientated by trees and hedges looming up suddenly at unexpected angles. Being surrounded by fog, we were in our own world that morning. Fog has a strange effect on the way sound carries, and we heard only the rushing of the Thames in enthusiastic mood and an occasional bird song. There was a feeling of complete peace and detachment from the human world, of just us with nature all to ourselves. Some bird resented having his Sunday peace disturbed by us humans and came flashing up from the river bank, then zig-zagged away into the fog before we could see what he was.

All good things come to an end. A V-notched stile took us up and over the embankment of the disused North Wiltshire canal. To our immediate left was a wooden bridleway bridge, built on the site of a former aqueduct over the Thames. To our right was a gate, leading on to the next field. One inch behind the gate were fifteen tons of bullocks, all crowded up to the gate, and looking most belligerent. "We don't have to go that way, do we?", said Big John. "Oh, yes we do!".

Big John and I had lately discussed fields full of cows. I am intimidated by them, he says they add to the atmosphere. (I'll agree with that!). So, Big John had to be the one to try. He squeezed through the gate, clapped his hands once or twice, and the beasts backed off to let him through. But as he progressed into the field, they closed in behind him, forming a ring around him, and it took him some while to leave them behind. Clearly, (and luckily for us three remaining humans) it was going to be difficult to get Ben-the-Dog through - he attracts cows like a bovine magnet - so Big John sneaked quite a long way down the old canal to find a place where we cowards could get through the fence un-noticed. Success! a scramble through the bed of the old canal, and a wriggle through the trees, and there we were, safe and sound. No, we weren't! Another bovine bulk appeared out of the gloom. I'm assured that Hereford bulls are not aggressive. With nowhere to hide except in the deep and very cold Thames, it's lucky this one wasn't.

The Thames Path doesn't strictly exist in these next fields - there is a permissive way courtesy of the farmer, which allowed us to stay on the river bank. The Thames water was clear, and fast flowing, and obviously several feet deep in parts - not a good place to fall in. We came to the last railway bridge over the Thames - a long-disused construction which carried the former line from Cirencester to Marlborough via Swindon. The poor old thing was tatty, but is still retained as a bridleway crossing. To David's double delight our path was under the bridge. Delight number one was the boggy, muddy riverbank. David enjoyed himself for a moment as only a young lad in wellies can. Delight number two was his first rest of the morning, perching on a stile and munching his muesli bar. Young John also found himself a moment of delight watching a number of trout deep in the water.

One more field brought us to another stile, where the farmer had used plenty of signs asking walkers to 'Keep to the Path', 'Don't Ride Bikes' and 'Please Wipe Your Feet'. We were requested to leave the river bank at this point, and after a short length of bridleway, we found a gravel track, clearly signposted to Ashton Keynes.

The next couple of miles really made it worthwhile being up and out this foggy, late autumn Sunday. The Thames Path is deviated deliberately from the river to make use of existing footpaths around the Cotswold Water Park. These wind initially between the Thames and a very waterlogged rough-ploughed field, passing the small stone-arched Bournelake bridge which was showing its age but remains useable. The footpath then leaves the river and takes a wandering line around Cleveland Lakes, a series of man-made lakes - flooded gravel pits - which have been allowed, with a little help, to return to nature. In the fog, which had lifted a bit but was still restricting vision to not much over 200 yards, it was easy to imagine we were on a remote Scottish lochside. We could hear, and just see, waterfowl both on the water and doing circuits and bumps, though it wasn't possible to see what sort of ducks or geese they were. Some peewits flew over, and somewhere overhead a swan also flew past, squeaking in a most eerie way - most disconcerting unless you know that swans wings need regular oiling. Though there were forty or fifty car parking spaces marked out, there were no cars at all, and we had these lakes to ourselves. On a clearer winter's day these lakes must be a bird-spotter's dream.

We rounded the first lake, then strolled on past a second. Another disturbed bird flew up from almost under our feet, and shot away, keeping low, darting left and right as it went. Long discussions followed before we decided it was a snipe, and so it was likely that the earlier similar disturbed bird had also been a snipe. There were signs of potential human activity, with a few rowing boats scattered inverted on the bank, and a toilet marked for 'Lady Anglers Only'. Now that explained why we'd hardly seen any lady anglers in all our walks - just one toilet provided for them along more than 70 miles of river.

The path then looped round a to a third lake which had extensive shallows around it. There was sign after sign telling us to 'Keep Out - Quicksand', yet there were hundreds of birds paddling, ignoring the signs completely. Obviously they were embarrassed at our finding them wading in contravention of the notices, because large gatherings of birds suddenly took flight. Their wings made such a noise in the still air that we simply stood and gawped. It was a sound all its own, unlike any other we'd ever heard, magnified by the fog. The nervousness of the nearest flock communicated itself to the rest of the lake, and we were treated to the tremendous sound and occasional sight of hundreds, maybe thousands, of peewits and other birds we couldn't identify in the gloom, wheeling about in great swirling clouds, flying towards us at one point, then splitting into two huge flocks that went left and right of us before turning back towards the lake again, in a marvellous flying display that lasted for five minutes and more. Now that was a treat and a half.

71

A most comprehensive signpost directed us towards Waterhay Bridge, and a quarter mile of walking brought us there. To celebrate seeing the free flying display, we had a CDM, (a bar of chocolate for younger readers) and the day's first nip of water-and-whiskey - which goes nicely with chocolate!

We were now obliged to leave the Thames for a while, as the designated Thames Path actually follows one of several other streams in the area. After a short length of road, we got back into a field, and picked up the line of the anonymous stream. Two fields onwards a very decrepit stone bridge gave us a means of carefully crossing the stream, and an obliging lady taking her dog for a Sunday stroll indicated the gap in the hedge leading us onward. The fog was thinning slightly, and we could see far enough to head accurately for a stile into Ashton Keynes cricket ground. By village standards, they had a very classy pavilion and pitch, very neatly kept, and not the slightest sign of typical sportsground tat and grot scattered anywhere. Only the clock, stuck at just after nine o'clock, let the place down (or perhaps it didn't - perhaps we really had walked 4 miles from Cricklade in five minutes?). Members of this cricket club must be very fit and supple. The exit from the ground was through a most wrigglesome stone stile with a horizontal upper bar - not something suited to the over-21's and dogs among us.

Without the guidebook, finding the next bit of the Thames Path would have been very hit-and-miss. We weaved our way round the tracks, fields and back roads of Ashton Keynes, eventually reaching the pub. It must have taken us nearly two and a half hours to walk the quarter mile from the cricket ground to here, as our watches now showed 11.30am. David pointed out that if we had dawdled a bit more, the pub would have been open.

Now, just prior to the pub we passed a wrecked Peugeot 309, parked on a driveway, presumably awaiting the insurance assessor, as this one looked well past the point of being salvageable. We had a Peugeot 309 not so long ago, but the family we sold it to had it written off when they were rammed by a drunken driver. I'm not sure if the lads were aware of the fate of their old car, so I mentioned it. Yes, they'd heard, and "Dad, who pays?". Over the next mile or more, my appreciation of the scenery was diminished by answering ever more convoluted points on insurance and compensation. Young John kept it straight-forward, but David got carried away.

"Dad". "Yes, David?". "If you are hit by a car that bounces into a tree which falls on your car doing more damage do you claim off the driver or the owner of the tree or both or can you claim double?". Had this question finished? No! "... and what if the other driver's car was faulty can you claim off the garage and claim three times and what if you die before you get the money and why is it cheaper to die than be injured?"

Ashton Keynes certainly was a picturesque Cotswold village, nearly attractive enough to act as a diversion from David's mind-twisting questioning. The footpath had brought us back alongside the Thames, which flows alongside the main street in a style reminiscent of Bourton-on-the-Water, with neat grassy banks to the river and equally neat personal bridges over the river here and there, leading to typical Cotswold stone buildings. Amazing to say, there were even several groups of people out for a Sunday stroll. The footpath continued upstream along by the Thames, passing between two cottages. One of them had a small notice in its window requesting "No parking", which seemed unnecessary until Big John spotted that the wall and window was actually a well-disguised garage door - only the hinges gave it away.

The next mile and a half (David's questioning apart) was a pure delight. The Thames flows between artificial embankments and the area is well cared for. It was more like walking along a canal towpath, especially having crossed a minor road to a long stretch where the bank has been built up with stakes and netting, and surfaced with gravel. With very easy walking, a strip of woods on one side, and a distant view through the thinning mist of another lake over the far bank, even the biggest concentration of other people we had seen since Oxford didn't spoil the pleasure.

The woods widened out and again we found lakes both sides of us - with a few fishermen. We met a pair of serious walkers - all 'good mornings' and walking boots - and then actually overtook a party of walkers who were sort-of going the same way as us, but had stopped at one part-filled lakes to watch the birdlife. One lady has an enormous telescope with her which might have been wonderful to use, but needed to be rested on something substantial (like a tree, or a husband) to stop it wobbling. We sneaked past them, then crossed the Thames over a small wooden footbridge. Big John wanted to take a photograph, so, professional posers that they are, David and Young John took the opportunity to have a rest - just avoiding dropping their wellies in the river as they did.

73

David was starting to complain about sore feet, and the next half mile, being on gravel and tarmac, were very hard on him, and I could hear his occasional sharp intakes of breath. We passed Lower Mill, where 'refreshments can sometimes be found', (but not that day, they couldn't, at which moment David's feet got instantly more tender), then soon afterwards we crossed the main road to reach Neigh Bridge Country Park. This was a bit of a grand name for a car park and a few benches, but it was all we needed. It was time for lunch.

The Thames Long Distance Path does not cater for the casual tripper - this was the first picnic area that we'd come across along the whole length from Goring. We made good use of it, for despite it being the first day of December it was warm enough for well-dressed walkers to sit at a picnic bench in relative comfort. The fog had thinned to a mist, letting us see just the outline of the midday sun, and the water in the lake was almost flat, creating a marvellous setting for a winter's picnic. David reminded me that I'd promised to check his sore feet for him. There were no cracks in his eczema, nor any blistering or signs of rubbing, so the best I could do for him was to put on him an extra layer of socks, hoping that two thicknesses would absorb some of the lumps for him.

Just as we got up to go, Big John produced the bag of sweets that hadn't seen daylight since Abingdon, sixty miles and six months previously. Getting the wrappers off had become a very tricky, sticky operation. Sucking on fruit sweets, and trying to get rid of the self-adhesive wrappers, we set off.

The path continued along the bank of the Thames, through a lovely wooded glade, but came to a violent end where some landowner had decided he couldn't cope with peasants on his precious land. We didn't care - the diversion along the head of a lake was just as nice. We passed a few fishermen who were less intense about their pastime than anglers we had observed previously - they were managing with much less clutter, and some of them were actually talking to each other. And for me, it was nice to hear a proper yokel accent again - the Gloucestershire speech hereabouts is very similar to my native Vale of Evesham ooo-aaarr speech.

A short length of road-walking followed, winding along a very narrow lane. We turned off just opposite a farm with two very bossy sheepdogs that defended their territory in a most aggressive and un-necessary manner. Being separated from them by a fairly secure gate, I barked back at them, which, for a moment at least, had them baffled. By the time they'd worked it out, we've gone over a stile into the next field. Mind you, we were not much better off there. Two donkeys had use of the field, and only a skinny fence separated them from us. I've never seen such energetic or noisy donkeys - they came galloping up to us making a noise Young John described as a hundred gates in need of oiling. I'm afraid we disappointed them. We gave them not one morsel (I doubt if we had much to give, anyway) and not trusting their teeth, I kept my fingers well hidden in my pockets.

The path passed right outside the door to one of the Kemble Mill cottages, and crossed the mill race over a wooden footbridge, hung on the side of the old mill building. A twisting path then went over the Thames proper, past a sluice gate which hadn't been moved in many a year, and then led us out into a large open field, with a well-trodden track across to the village of Somerford Keynes. Away to our left - that's west, roughly - the line of the Thames showed as the lowest point of a very broad, shallow valley, with just an impression of Cotswold fields in the mist beyond.

There was a group of three buildings, tithe barn, manor house and church, all in grey limestone, facing onto the next field we reached. On a sunny day they would make an imposing photo. That day they didn't. Strange, though, how these three buildings, surely the focus of village life once upon a time, were actually isolated somewhat from the rest of the village. A wicket gate led to a very shady pathway around the church (though who needed shade on a day like this?). Passing a holly tree I could see that it's true that only the lower leaves of this plant are spiked, the higher leaves, well out of reach of cattle, have a more normal oval shape. It was a good job for the tree that there are no giraffes in Somerford Keynes.

David had been asking whether this village had a pub and could we go. Luckily I was spared any arguments as the route turned across a field before we got to the village street, where I just happened to know there was a pub. I was very conscious of having to keep to time. Even now the light was starting to fail, we still had the best part of four miles to go and we had not left a car at the end of the walk, but arranged for Anne to drive out and meet us. I didn't want to keep her waiting.

Lifting Ben-the-Dog across yet another stile, we followed a Gloucestershire County Council footpath sign pointing vaguely across a field. Our guidebook promised a 'very narrow squeeze stile' at the end of the field. It was right - the stile was only just child size - good job the farm gate was open! Several fields of level walking got us towards Upper Mill farm. Although the path here follows the general line of the Thames, we were kept away from the river bank and followed the line of the hedges at the top of the fields. There was one interruption when David felt a desperate need to answer the call of nature. But, when I mentioned the lack of Andrex in my rucksack, he decided that perhaps he could ignore nature a while longer. Have we brought our children up to expect every comfort in life?

The final stile before Upper Mill Farm was followed immediately by a single strand electric fence, so we paused and thought about it before climbing very tentatively over, not wishing to be zapped into oblivion. We boldly decided it was not to keep walkers out, but to stop animals reaching a ditch alongside the stile, and we boldly stepped over it. Soon we reached the site of the Upper Mill. The mill race was still there, and it was possible to see where the undershot water wheel had been pivoted. David, with memories of Thorpe Park (a sort of Home Counties Disneyland) in his mind, would like to take a boat down this vicious little waterslide one day. Not me, thankyou! We followed the Thames itself now. The next few hundred yards of path had a footing of limestone and rubble, which surprisingly made for rather harder walking than mud or grass. It was a relief to get back into the open fields that followed, with the Thames on our right looking again more like a canal than a river. (How observant of me! This 'river' is actually the old mill channel, which now carries all the Thames water flowing at this point.)

A row of electricity pylons slant across this valley, and so I asked the lads how come birds can perch on the cables. "Plastic feet", they said. (Ask a stupid question, I thought.) But the question did strike a chord with them, as both lads intelligently discussed with me power transmission, insulation, and electrocution, though David went rather further, hypothesising that a lightning conducter buried in an appropriate field would produce instant roast spuds, or instant roast beef. The thought of plastic feet had also got through to David's legs, which, encased in rubber wellies (very similar to plastic), had taken to leaping into cowpats again. The weather being damp, and the fields being boggy, these pats were very slippy and fluid, and were coming an awfully long way up his wellies. Young John, more interested in things living, spotted a couple of grey squirrels shinning very rapidly up a tree. We were not near any woodland, there being merely the odd scattered tree here and there, and he wondered what they found to eat.

Talking of things slippy and fluid, we turned away from the river for a spell, to follow an imaginary footpath across two boggy fields. Almost immediately something fast and flying zapped away from almost under our feet. It was probably another snipe - they were like buses that day, nothing for thirty-nine years and then three come along all at once. This field was well waterlogged, with water lying many inches deep in places. This was a real test of Claire's waterproofing compound, and it really did work - my feet stayed dry. (Of course, if it hadn't worked, gentleman that I am, I would never have mentioned it at all.) Two more fields, and countless more cowpats, brought us to the end of the bogginess, and gave us a chance to rest our weary bones on the parapet of a road bridge over the Thames.

We were on the edge of Ewen, and David again started to raise the subject of going to the pub. On a late autumn afternoon, with the gloom getting ever so slightly thicker, and my legs definitely feeling the strain, there was nothing I'd like more than to be in a pub, taking long, comforting draughts of Guinness, sitting in front of a roaring log fire and watching the pictures in the flames. And I'd like it so much, I could imagine myself sitting there all day and all night. So we didn't.

Half a mile of road walking took us away from the Thames for a spell, going in, then out, of Ewen, and then down to Parker's bridge where we picked up the line of the Thames again. David and Young John both complained of being footsore, so Big John mollified them with the last of the boiled sweets, and I generously let them take a final break at the bridge. By this time the light was noticeably fading and I wanted to get to the source in daylight, so I grabbed David's hand and away we went. From this point upstream, we had riverbank walking all the way to the source, and I seemed to get a second wind now the end of the project was in sight.

The next half-mile of the Thames was narrow, but carried a tremendous volume of rushing, deep, clear water. Big John found this the most impressive part of the entire river, especially as we were less than a mile from the spring at Lyd Well.

We carefully crossed the A429 leading to Kemble at the site of the last road bridge on the Thames. This was also the site of a former railway crossing, though that bridge has long gone and the embankment has been chopped well back from the road. I had been here a few weeks previously, looking for possible parking places. At that time, at the end of a long dry summer, there was no water at all in the Thames channel, and I was able to walk on a season's growth of grass on what should have been the river bed. November's rain had made a tremendous difference, and even this close to the spring, the Thames upstream of the bridge was now a vigorous stream, some ten feet wide and much, much deeper than a child's welly.

Having walked (or limped or creaked according to our preferences) a little way into the field we could see the wind-driven water pump which is sited at the spring known as Lyd Well that in practice feeds the Thames. We made a supreme effort to get there quickly. Like the river itself, this spring had been dry just a few weeks back. Now it was bubbling up strongly from the depths of a black hole, the water coming out so strongly that it formed a noticeable dome above above the level of the sizable pool from which the infant Thames was flowing. According to some maps, this is the source of the River Thames, and is certainly the uppermost point with any significant flow of water. It was disappointing to find no monument or plaque or marker stone, and no easy way of viewing this impressive spring. It deserves better.

And now for the last leg. (A good job, too - I was already on mine). Although Lyd Well is undoubtedly where the first significant waters come from, the official true source of the Thames is another mile onwards. Believe me, you have to have a lot of faith in a guidebook to follow a damp ditch which rapidly becomes just a dry watercourse and finally, after a feeble and pointless attempt at a stone footbridge, becomes pure imagination. There was a pool of water at the top end of the field, but it would have had to flow uphill to get into the Thames from there. In one corner of the field was a ditch, surrounded by barbed wire, that could be the line of the watercourse. This field and ditch came to an abrupt end at an embankment carrying the Fosse Way. Access to the Fosse was by a series of stone steps up to a stile, and then a rapid traffic-avoiding dash (difficult with stiff legs and sore feet) got us to the relative safety of a farm gateway.

We humans had no trouble with the stile, but perhaps Ben-the-Dog was feeling the strain a bit, as he collected four faults for refusing to take either the stile or to slip between the bars of the gate. It took a little ingenuity to find him enough gap in the combination hedge and fence. "Just two more fields, lads", I told them, all false jollity and enthusiasm. An easy farm track took us to the access to the next field. There was one of those big stepladder affairs to get over the dry stone wall, but our gratitude went to the farmer who had left the adjacent gate wide open just for us.

Now, the source was reputed to be in a 'grove of trees'. There was nothing to be seen nearby, so we plodded towards the distant end, and also towards a herd of cattle that were being let in to 'our' field way off in the far corner. I was eyeing up the distance to the fence in case the cows decide to visit, when suddenly, materialising out of the gloom, I saw the stone that marked the end. Poor old David was genuinely struggling now, and needed some help to get there. "Is that it?", he wanted to know, sounding most miffed."All this way to see a stone?".

Thameshead, the official source at Trewsbury Mead, was an anti-climax. There was no water at all - there had been no sign of a watercourse at all for the last quarter mile - all we found was a ring of little bits of limestone around a hole that might have been a spring once. The marker was a large lump of granite, with a barely readable inscription, in memory of the Thames Commissioners from 1857 to 1974, for some illegible reason. This being a large and solid piece of rock, we could safely lean on it - and I certainly needed to. Like all good explorers we took photographs of each other, (using flash lighting, it was so dark), and then also like all good explorers, we turned round and went back. Having completed the Thames Path, there was nothing left to drive us on, (even the cows weren't threatening us), and it was very hard to get the legs working to return to the main road. Contrary Ben-the-Dog nipped easily through the gate that caused him anguish on the way up - perhaps he knew he was going home. Big John had a sudden pair of thoughts. The bad news was that we forgot to celebrate our success at the stone with a nip of water-and-whiskey. The good news was that because of this oversight, there was some mixture left in his hip flask - but not for long!

200 yards of careful stumbling along the verge next to the horribly fast traffic on the Fosse Way got us to the lay-by where Anne was going to meet us. Would you believe it - we were ten minutes early, giving us plenty of time to dispose of a second bar of chocolate. We waited and waited, then we waited a bit more, then lots of bits more, and finally a whole lot of more, before my nearest and dearest turned up. Would you believe it - she knew we'd never keep to schedule, so she timed her journey to arrive about half an hour late! But, like I said, I never argue with a woman.

And Finally....

Every book I've read about the Thames - and I've read a few since starting this walk - has glossed over the Thames above Oxford, dismissing it in relatively few words, concentrating on the downstream glories of the Thames such as London and Windsor. Even Jerome K. Jerome's Three Men in a Boat only went up as far as Oxford.

The fact we chose to walk along what I've called the Upper Thames was originally a matter of convenience. From the Goring gap up as far as Oxford, we found very much what we expected - broad sweeps of water, green meadows, and riverside towns such as Abingdon. Central Oxford itself was also much what a cynical local might expect. What other major tourist centre would fail to make good use of the riverside, and fail to direct the tourists to it? I'm sure that most foreign tourists leave Oxford without any idea that the country's most famous river flows right through the centre.

In our view, the best part of the Thames is upstream of Godstow. From here onwards there are no towns or villages on the river until Lechlade - just open country dotted with the occasional lock or pub. For the walker the Upper Thames Valley is a twenty-five mile corridor of remarkably isolated country-side, only a few miles and yet a world away from industrial, commercial, commuter-belt Oxfordshire. Not that this corridor of isolation is untamed countryside by any means - it would be surprising if a lowland river valley had remained untouched by human hand. This is managed, farmed, gentle country-side. This is essentially English countryside.

The county boundary between Oxfordshire and Gloucestershire at Lechlade marks a further change in the character of the Thames. Upstream of Lechlade, the limit of navigation, such glimpses of the Thames as we could get showed a much-diminished stream which, rather than dominating the scenery, becomes an integral part of it.

The thirteen miles of the Thames from Cricklade up to the spring at Lyd Well and on to the source at Thameshead turned out to be the best single day's walking either Big John or I have ever had. Though these bits of Wiltshire and Gloucestershire could hardly be described as remote, the towns and major

80

roads are sufficently far away as to be totally out of sight - and hence out of mind. The infant Thames, which is never more than a stream and reduces to, at best, a deep brook near the source, is simply a route-marker and an excuse for a delightfully varied journey around the lakes and through the fields and villages of the Cotswolds.

It has to be said that we enjoyed ourselves. What started out as a walk of convenience turned out to be a wonderful experience and, for us, a journey of discovery. Despite blisters and aching legs, despite rampant vegetation and belligerent cattle, despite impassable footpaths and long miles of road work, despite rain and wind and heat and fog, we enjoyed it. We achieved our goal of walking to the source of the Thames, and in doing so we found for ourselves a glorious bit of English countryside - right on our doorstep.

Recent TV programmes have gone in search of the 'real' England. It's still to be found along the Upper Thames Valley - meadows, cows, wildlife, country pubs and peace are all here. Of course, reality is here too - electric fences, scratchy bushes, pill boxes and pylons - but if you select the view carefully, close one eye and squint a bit, you can still find rural England.

No, walking the Upper Thames Path didn't make my body fit, but it did wonders for my soul.